ROUTLEDGE LIBRARY EDITIONS: MARRIAGE

Volume 9

MARRIED TO MELANESIA

.

MARRIED TO MELANESIA

MURIEL JONES

LONDON AND NEW YORK

First published in 1974 by George Allen & Unwin Ltd.

This edition first published in 2023
by Routledge
4 Park Square, Milton Park, Abingdon, Oxon OX14 4RN

and by Routledge
605 Third Avenue, New York, NY 10158

Routledge is an imprint of the Taylor & Francis Group, an informa business

© 1974 George Allen & Unwin Ltd.

All rights reserved. No part of this book may be reprinted or reproduced or utilised in any form or by any electronic, mechanical, or other means, now known or hereafter invented, including photocopying and recording, or in any information storage or retrieval system, without permission in writing from the publishers.

Trademark notice: Product or corporate names may be trademarks or registered trademarks, and are used only for identification and explanation without intent to infringe.

British Library Cataloguing in Publication Data
A catalogue record for this book is available from the British Library

ISBN: 978-1-032-46071-0 (Set)
ISBN: 978-1-032-48680-2 (Volume 9) (hbk)
ISBN: 978-1-032-48685-7 (Volume 9) (pbk)
ISBN: 978-1-003-39025-1 (Volume 9) (ebk)

DOI: 10.4324/9781003390251

Publisher's Note
The publisher has gone to great lengths to ensure the quality of this reprint but points out that some imperfections in the original copies may be apparent.

Disclaimer
The publisher has made every effort to trace copyright holders and would welcome correspondence from those they have been unable to trace.

MARRIED
TO
MELANESIA

by
MURIEL JONES

Illustrated by Ken Watkinson

London
GEORGE ALLEN & UNWIN LTD
Ruskin House   Museum Street

First published in 1974

This book is copyright under the Berne Convention. All rights are reserved. Apart from any fair dealing for the purpose of private study, research, criticism or review, as permitted under the Copyright Act, 1956, no part of this publication may be reproduced, stored in a retrieval system, or transmitted, in any form or by any means, electronic, electrical, chemical, mechanical, optical, photocopying, recording or otherwise, without the prior permission of the copyright owner. Enquiries should be addressed to the publishers.

© George Allen & Unwin Ltd. 1974

ISBN 0 04 910056 4

Printed in Great Britain
in 12 point Fournier type
by Cox & Wyman Ltd
London, Fakenham and Reading

CONTENTS

I	*South Seas Impact*	page 9
II	*Siota*	14
III	*Mother, Father and Aunt Jane*	27
IV	*David*	35
V	*Moving*	42
VI	*New Home*	52
VII	*Students*	62
VIII	*Friends and Neighbours*	71
IX	*Religion*	84
X	*Beasts*	95
XI	*Botanical*	113
XII	*'In Journeyings Oft . . .'*	123
XIII	*Honiara*	136
XIV	*Change*	149

ILLUSTRATIONS

Map of the Solomon Islands	*page*	8
Siota		21
'. . . a splendid little house . . . approached by a coral causeway'		24
David being helpful and friendly to the ladies of Minnesota		40
Everything came ashore		50
Kohimarama		53
The crocodile pool at Tanaemba		96
Road to Honiara		130
China Town, Honiara		138
Within a Chinese emporium		140

Map of the Solomon Islands

I

SOUTH SEAS IMPACT

About eighteen months after our marriage, which took place in December 1968, we read an article in *Time* magazine about the psychological dangers of too much change in the life of any individual in too short a time. Personal changes were graded on a scale of gravity and potential damage. Marriage, bereavement and divorce scored heavily. Changing one's job, moving from one city to another or simply to a new house were less serious, but each added its quota to the total and anybody working up too high a score in any one year was advised to watch it and take things gently. We found that we had easily broken the psychological bank before we had started on the numerous major changes that they did not even list.

We were married after three years at opposite ends of the world, too near Christmas for convenience, and spent what was left of our honeymoon – after we had changed our wills, rearranged our banking and insurance, put ourselves as right as anybody ever is with the Inland Revenue Department and our property into our joint name – attending family funerals. Marriage and bereavement. We then, too rapidly for comfort, made off in a snowstorm for the South Seas, to a change of climate, diet and whole manner of life. All this we imprudently did in our late forties.

I had, as I thought, retired from my tropical career after sixteen years in Africa before I met my husband, who was at the time about to start his (if you do not count the war) in the

9

Married to Melanesia

relatively benign conditions of Suva, the agreeable and civilised capital of Fiji. Three years later, we were married in England and embarking on a major adventure in the Solomon Islands, where Eric had been persuaded by a new and reforming Bishop of Melanesia to attempt a dramatic *aggiornamento* in the education and training of clergymen and other church workers.

The Pacific was a completely new world to me, but it was hard not to see it in African terms; the vegetation was similar to that of the lusher parts of tropical Africa, familiar coconut palms waved over the beaches, zinnias proliferated in the European gardens of the capital, the people were much the same in colour and outward appearance, and the British raj manifested itself in traditional Public Works procedures and much else. Politically, it felt like an excessively old-fashioned colonial situation, but one with many familiar features. Had Eric simply brought me back with him to Suva, which we visited on our way to Honiara, I should have been wrong, but not so far wrong. Fiji, on the brink of independence, had certain similarities with African situations I had known and the people, especially the women, have always recalled to me the enterprise and dignity and some of the merriment of the Ghanaians who were my friends. But the Solomons proved very different and very daunting – until one got to know and like and faintly to understand the place and the people and the influences that have shaped them.

The impact – as the man writing in *Time* would have predicted – was traumatic, perhaps just because we were not in our first youth or innocent of other tropical experience. Many were the times that we looked at each other in dismay, middle-aged VSOs or Peace Corps, set down in a situation that would have been entertaining in one's early twenties but often became alarming and exhausting in one's late forties. Such was our first 'feast' in our first June. We now understand about feasts, partly through experience and partly because we have read some anthropology of the area and realise that they are not simply occasions of enjoyment but have a long history as the basis of

South Seas Impact

economic as well as social life and were, in the old days, as much the serious 'business' of a man as a job in the City might be in London. What is very interesting is the degree to which this seriousness about feasts has been carried over into the Christian era of these islands. The dedication day of the village church now prescribes the date of the village feast and church services are of central importance in the proceedings, but the feast itself is still that village's day for display; no invitations are sent, but everybody for miles around knows there will be a feast and makes a point of being present.

Our college was dedicated to St Peter and we quickly became aware that St Peter's Day was the culmination of its year. Religious services, football, netball, dancing (folk or, as we put it, 'custom'), a traditional feast, more dancing, more religion, and finally a tra-la-la (European-style dancing with guitars and Solomon Islands 'pop') occupied every moment from half past six in the morning to midnight and after. The students and their wives had been busy for days before, and the two previous nights had been devoted either to fishing or cooking the food in the earth ovens which had been prepared for the occasion. A pig had been bought some time earlier and fattened. Unluckily, it got wind of its impending doom and broke loose a few hours before it could be slaughtered and we were faced with the terrible shame of a feast without a pig. The students wore themselves out searching for it – we were worried not only by the loss but by the thought of dreadful bills for compensation, as it would undoubtedly be wrecking people's gardens – but to no avail. Money had to be scraped up from somewhere and a substitute pig, much smaller and inferior, to be found, bought and killed.

At this stage, we Europeans (ourselves and our colleagues, a young couple from New Zealand) were mainly helpless spectators while the customary activities rolled along with the momentum of tradition. But it soon became obvious to me that there would be visitors – *many* visitors – some of whom might need more in the way of food and shelter than the

Married to Melanesia

students could provide. I was still unreconciled at that point to life without a telephone or much of a postal service, where one might be catering for one meal or three days, for two people or for fifty, and I was a little startled when two enormous canoes put in to our beach as the sun set on the eve of the festival bearing a large party of schoolgirls with their teachers, including some young New Zealanders, who had come for the feast. But all were eventually fed and bedded down and we awaited the dawn, when we were invaded by villagers from the whole island, the Bishop and his party in the *Southern Cross* (the Bishop's small ship), many more canoe-loads, another diocesan ship, a European yachtsman from Honiara who had been persuaded to give a lift in his trimaran to various young women – in fact, as Solomons' pidgin expressively puts it, 'olgeta' (a word which seems to derive from 'altogether' and forms a universal plural).

Meanwhile, the rain came down and nobody took the slightest notice. We had a church service, we had a series of football matches, the Mothers' Union surprisingly (to me) played netball matches, everybody did 'custom' dances by island groups, the rain lifted a bit and we sat on the ground in the open around palm-frond 'tablecloths' to charred pig, fish, and 'pudding', a rich, baked concoction of coconut, cassava, and so on, very dense of texture, very filling and, as far as I can discover, almost peculiar to feasts. Everything is done up in parcels of banana leaf, which makes it a lucky dip. Earth-oven-baked fish can be delicious; so can baked pork. But all too often one unwinds one's parcel to disclose a head with fishy eyes gazing at one, or a piece of succulent pig fat. Speeches were made and songs sung. The songs traditional at these feasts are very *sui generis* and range from 'Ilkley Moor baht 'at' and 'One man went to mow' to a taunt song in pidgin, left over from the Japanese Occupation in the Second World War, of which the only words I have ever been able to catch are 'Japoni, ha-ha!'; this one is often accompanied with dance and mime.

Having sat down to eat, we rose up, like the Children of

South Seas Impact

Israel, to play, but with deplorably little digestive pause. More dancing. More religion. More eating. Tra-la-la. Relentless rain. My day seemed made up of slipping bits of food and drink to those whose stomachs could not take the festal public fare. Certainly, a nice cup of tea is a life-saver on these occasions. The more distinguished guests departed in their ships. It still rained – and now the wind got up too. The young were dancing in the dining-hall to the strains of guitars and the single men were no doubt enjoying the unusual pleasure of female society – the visiting schoolgirls and their teachers. We put in an appearance but soon retired to bed, exhausted by the day and marvelling at Melanesian energy. It rained harder than ever and the wind howled round the house. The last thing we heard, around midnight, was the girls embarking in their canoes with merry cries, setting off to cross a dozen miles of rough sea and be in class by half past seven next morning. We shuddered, hoped they would not drown and thought – as so often – rather them than us. Next time we saw the teachers, some weeks later, they told us that one of the canoes had indeed turned over but the girls had swum along and righted it and got in again.

It was, we decided, a tough country where even pleasures are strenuously won and strenuously enjoyed. In what other tropical country do people play football at midday? Is there anywhere else in the Anglican world where the Mothers' Union round off their meetings with a netball match? And our mothers, unlike many of their fellow-members elsewhere, are practising mothers, still in the process of producing an annual baby.

II

SIOTA

Siota, where we spent our first Melanesian year, is on the smallish island of Gela or Florida. Until the Second World War, the British administration, such as it was, was centred in Tulagi on Gela, but after the war a new capital grew up around the airstrip, the few miles of road and the Quonset huts left by the American forces at Honiara on Guadalcanal. Gela lost its administrative importance and has, in fact, fallen behind many of the other islands in development. Siota was at one time the headquarters of the Anglican diocese, but these had been moved, before our time, to the new capital and the only thing left at Siota was St Peter's College, training priests to serve the whole diocese which covers not only the Solomon Islands but parts of the New Hebrides. We had a fantasy that, just as theological colleges in England have a tendency to be established in quiet villages without much of a bus-service, presumably to make the young men mind their step and keep them unspotted from the world, St Peter's, being in the Solomon Islands where everything seems so extreme, was carefully set on a desert island, well away from shipping routes. We knew this was not true, but it felt true. The college was the only thing at Siota. Within walking distance were one or two tiny villages of up to ten houses each and also the very big village of Belaga, with a population of perhaps five hundred people and a church but – at that time – no school and no store. The only post office on the entire island was at Tulagi and so difficult of access that I never visited it in the course of the whole year. We ourselves did most of the postal business – quite informally – at our end

Siota

of the island and I have never ceased to be surprised that so many letters actually reach their destinations, though it may take them three months or so to make their way from one island to another and then from one village to another.

The Gela people are subsistence farmers and fishermen, living mainly on root vegetables, fish and coconuts. They make a little copra, which is the only source of cash for most people. Small ships operated by Chinese traders visit the villages every few weeks buying copra and selling a limited range of goods – calico, fish hooks, tinned meat and the like. This is the limit of the cash economy as far as most people are concerned, though enough money is made and saved by some communities and some individuals to buy a small outboard motor (a 'Seagull') which they fit to a traditional canoe, thereby becoming immensely mobile. Since we have lived on Guadalcanal, I have occasionally met Father Robert, who used to be our district priest when we were at Siota on the far side of Gela and asked him how he came across, on the *Southern Cross* or some other diocesan ship? 'Oh no,' he usually says, 'my Seagull.' It is a nasty, choppy stretch of ocean and I have often been seasick crossing it in a proper ship. It is also shark-infested.

In our time, Siota was on no regular shipping route. We were visited, unpredictably, by the diocese's small ships, Chinese copra boats, passing canoes and American round-the-world yachtsmen. Mail arrived as and when ships came. One of my most vivid recollections of Siota is of hearing a shout from the beach in the dark and rushing down with a lamp. It would be Father Robert, passing through with his 'Seagull'. We would help him to beach his canoe and take him up to the house for a cup of coffee while the students struggled up with a damp mailbag full of mail for 'olgeta', letters for unknown villagers which were dropped in a box on our office door and always seemed to disappear, letters from home for the students – who had often been longer away from their own island than we had – letters from England and Australia and New Zealand ('big place' in the local parlance), lots of business

Married to Melanesia

correspondence, and four-month-old numbers of the *New Statesman* or *The Observer* full of sage prediction about the political future which, by now and even for us – for we heard the BBC Overseas Service – was the past.

Our own link with the outside world was a 'speed-boat', which had been given to the mission station to help with medical emergencies. In this, we could get 'down the Passage' to the little mission hospital at Taroaniara, ten miles away, where there was no doctor but an English sister, Christine Woods, of tremendous character and forty years' experience of the Solomons. From Taroaniara, it was possible to be conveyed, at need, over more sea to the government station at Tulagi which was served by a twice-weekly government ship. A visit to the dentist in Honiara had to be long premeditated and a week allowed for it. If one was ill enough to see a doctor, one was, on the whole, too ill to be subjected to several hours of sun or rain in an open boat, a probable night *en route* and an arrival at the Central Hospital in Honiara without notice, after they had packed up for the day and might well not have an empty bed. I tried this once and decided to die quietly in my own bed at home in future. Our predecessor's wife actually had a baby on a diocesan ship in mid-ocean in an attempt to be decently delivered in the Central Hospital.

Nonie, the wife of Eric's only colleague, George Connor from New Zealand, was luckily a trained and highly competent and enterprising nurse and we leaned heavily on her in all ordinary medical, and indeed veterinary, emergencies. When the Connors went on leave during our first September, we realised just how much the whole island relied on her. Missionaries are plainly expected to marry nurses; it could not be understood that I – the only European woman within reach – had no special medical competence and Eric and I were soon operating a very amateur clinic on our verandah, dressing ulcers and injuries, pouring anti-malarial drugs down the protesting throats of sometimes dying babies, and doing whatever common sense suggested. When we were beat, we sent them

Siota

down the Passage in the 'speed-boat' to Christine Woods, but this made heavy inroads both on our petrol ration and on time, because a student had to be withdrawn from his studies to drive the boat.

These experiences taught us a lot. Life on a South Sea island sounds idyllic and the colour photos are certainly pretty. Western city-dwellers deprecate civilisation's 'interference' with the Wordsworthian simplicity of people's lives, but the people of Gela, as we knew them, would have welcomed a great deal of 'interference' in the form of medical services and communications. The infant mortality was appalling and the level of health and efficiency among adults was pretty low on account of the endemic malaria. Lives were unnecessarily lost because of the difficulty of getting sick or injured people, or women in obstructed labour to the hospital. From one point of view, they were at least better off than their great-grandparents. Nobody was afraid to walk from village to village, for clan warfare, cannibalism and the blood feud were things of the past; and this is almost entirely attributable to the influence of the Church. Life has improved for the people even since we left Gela in 1970. The World Health Organisation's malaria eradication programme is having a dramatic success and should save the lives of many babies and raise the whole level of health and energy of the people. A regular shipping service now keeps Siota and Belaga in touch with the capital and people are even finding it worth their while to grow produce to sell in the Honiara market.

In 1969, nothing seemed to be grown for sale except coco-nuts for copra, and one of our greatest privations was the lack of fresh food. True, we arrived soon after a cyclone and it was some months before the devastated gardens could be replanted and come into bearing. After this interval, beans, tomatoes, pawpaws and the occasional pineapple were brought to our door. Money was not very useful. The universal coinage was local tobacco, rich and tarry. I used to keep a smelly box of this in the bottom of my wardrobe and barter it, a stick at a time,

Married to Melanesia

for a bundle of beans. Occasionally somebody would beg a cupful of sugar instead. I once parted with some dried milk to a pathetic widower who had walked ten miles to try to get something for a motherless infant (young widowers were distressingly frequent, maternal mortality being what it was). And at Christmas my heart was touched by a woman who had brought a pineapple many miles in the hope that the Europeans would take it in exchange for any kind of toy for her little boy. I was delighted that I happened to have a rubber ball in the house to barter.

Before my residence on Gela I had never conceived of a tropical place where markets were not held to dispose of local produce, and I gaily left Honiara on our first arrival thinking bananas, pawpaws, beans, and so on would be locally available for money. As a result of the cyclone, it was two or three months before we saw so much as a banana. The first bundle of beans I greeted as a direct intervention of the Lord who sent ravens to feed Elijah in the wilderness. Indeed, from that time to this, our domestic word for somebody selling something at the door has been a 'raven'. During our year at Siota, only two small markets were held in the neighbouring village, both on a Saturday afternoon and both within a single month. We never discovered why they were held just then or how people knew they were to be held. We simply saw canoes converging on the beach, grabbed a basket and our money, and ran down. We were even able to buy fresh fish, a luxury we only otherwise enjoyed when a student caught some and gave us a present.

Most of our food had to come out of tins – a dismal introduction to my career as a housewife. We had arrived in Honiara on a Wednesday afternoon. A diocesan ship was laid on to take us together with the new students and the Connors, who had a new baby, over to Siota on the Friday. Thursday was the only opportunity for our necessary business, banking and shopping. We bought soap and toilet rolls and a sack of sugar and tins of dried milk, fish, etc., by the boxful. Corned beef

Siota

and tinned steak were obvious necessities. Eric advised against Australian corned beef; the words, he said, had a different significance in the antipodes and we should not like it. Then we found a French brand. We had never heard the name, but the French, we reasoned, care about what they eat, so we bought two crates of it, ninety-six tins. All was sent down to the wharf and we set sail with our supplies.

The first evening at Siota we ate with the Connors, already experienced and organised island-dwellers, a delicious meal of roast pork brought over from the Honiara butchery. They warned us that this might well be our last meal of fresh meat for the next three months. Next day we unpacked – and confronted our tins. Our first impression of the corned beef was that it was totally inedible – definitely an export product which no Frenchman in his senses would touch. The steak and onions was next broached and proved, if anything, more nauseating, floating as it all was in a sickly, yellowish mass of near-rancid fat. This left the fish – large tins of 'mackerel-style', Lenten (it *was* actually Lent) but edible. Brand-name 777.

Bread was baked every second day by the students in an ingenious oven contrived from empty 44-gallon oil-drums and earth. It was usually very good, except towards the end of the quarter, when the flour was pretty damp and weevil-ridden, or when the students forgot the salt (Melanesians do not seem to care as much as we do about salt) or when the baking team had just changed and had not quite learnt its trade. So our most delicious meals were, in fact, 777 sandwiches.

But the meat was a challenge. We had chilli powder, various herbs and plenty of curry powder in the house (through an oversight in reading a catalogue, I had ordered enough curry powder to make a twice-weekly curry for the next hundred years). I used to wake up in the night wondering what could possibly be done to disguise the flavour of the corned beef, but whatever I did the original old horse won. The stewed steak and onions was, if anything, more of a problem. Eric had the intelligent idea of heating it so that the unspeakable fat might

Married to Melanesia

float to the top, then chilling it and scraping off the grease. So, one early evening, we lit the kerosene burners under the tin box which did duty for an oven, put in seven or eight tins of steak and onions and went out for ten minutes to enjoy one of our simple pleasures, watching the sunset from the end of our jetty and lying on our stomachs to gaze down on to the incredible shoals of little jewel-coloured fishes swimming around underneath – a tropical fish-tank immensely magnified. All was very still and balmy and we were smoking a contented cigarette when there was a loud explosion from the direction of our house. We leaped up and rushed back, to find steak and onions and its grease all over the kitchen as well as the oven. We did not really regret the loss of the food, but the smell lingered on and was hard to live with.

The corned beef problem also solved itself. We ordered some better tinned food from England, which arrived in three or four months, and also, at the end of two months, had occasion to go to Honiara with a bit more leisure to look round and find something eatable. We also brought back with us a charming female kitten who had been reared in the house of the Attorney-General, so he said, on the cheaper kinds of locally-available tinned meat. She seemed not to object to the French corned horse and ate her way steadily through a crate and a half. When she was within three tins of the finishing line, unfortunately, she went out to dinner with the Connor cats, three bachelor brothers who kept a monastery next door and had taken up with her enthusiastically; she returned claiming to have discovered that cats eat cat-food. After this, she refused any further dealings with the French and we had to order her a crate of 'Tucker Box' from Australia.

The Siota house was, I thought, rather pleasant. Eric had seen it before our marriage on a visit from Fiji, and had described it to me with some misgivings as a sort of cricket pavilion. It was an old-fashioned mission bungalow on stilts, rather crudely constructed by an enterprising amateur who had left all the woodwork unplaned and then painted over it, leav-

Siota

Married to Melanesia

ing it impossible to clean. The floor of the entire house was made from enormously long planks, very springy. I did not mind this, but Eric found it irritatingly noisy and was roused to frenzy when I moved about or tried to cook on Sunday mornings, thereby disturbing the record-player and making the playing-head jump.

We had some splendid lengths of tapa cloth, the traditional Polynesian bark-cloth (not characteristic of the Melanesian Solomon Islands), which Eric had acquired on a visit to Tonga in the train of the Bishop of Polynesia on the occasion of an ordination. Acres of the stuff had been made and ceremonially presented and Eric had come in for some of the loot as a by-stander. The royal arms of Tonga done in bark-cloth are not particularly pleasing and one felt they needed a chair of state to be placed under them, but we hung them over the worst places in the spare bedroom. The rest of the cloth was pleas-antly decorated with traditional designs and also some writing which we thought might be about ordination, but we could not understand it, nor could any of our guests or students, so it was easy to accept it as more design. The colour was a dark cream with brown patterns; this and the slightly hairy-yet-smooth texture always put me in mind of a nice cow. Anyway, we hung it around our living room as a sort of arras, and the effect was rich and strange and not unpleasing. It covered up some of the crudities of the woodwork and provided a happy nesting-place for the cockroaches.

There was a large veranda on which I set up my desk and did much of my teaching. It had a magnificent view of the sea and mountains, and one could look out for shipping or canoes while waiting for the students to think, which was often a laborious process that it was unwise to over-stimulate. It was distinctly awash with rain when it did rain, but this applied to the whole house. Our predecessors were said to have gone to bed in oilskins on occasions, but this, if true, was silly of them because if one bedroom was wet the other was probably moderately dry.

Siota

The principal drawback was really the absence of mod. cons. The cooking arrangements once or twice reduced me to tears, being not only primitive but nearly worn out (our experiments with the steak and onions did not improve them). There had been four kerosene burners, but by our time only two would work and these finally rusted through and fell to pieces three days before we left the house for good. They were never easy to light, so, once lit, they were used for all they were worth and one tended to live on a system of vacuum-flasks. Not that I ever reached the point of living as some nuns I once stayed with in Tanzania seemed to do. They were so highly organised with their flasks that even when they had a kettle boiling on a new fire, they were drinking instant coffee made with water from a flask from the last fire.

There was as splendid a bathroom (and with such a magnificent sunset view over the sea) as I have ever seen on a Melanesian mission station, with a six-foot bath in sparkling porcelain. Unfortunately, there was never water enough to use it as it was meant to be used, and certainly no question of hot water. But there was also a shower from a small cistern filled by a hand-operated pump. The water for this, however, came from the smallest of our roof-tanks, which was often dry, whereas the more useful shower – in the garden – was directly supplied from a bigger tank overhead. Eric always used this one. It was sketchily screened by a bit of corrugated iron, rather like a French street urinal. Visitors pretty well had to use it because the grand bathroom opened directly out of our bedroom, but I normally drew the line, partly because it really did seem a bit public and partly because I could hardly go down there naked and there was nowhere dry where one could leave a garment. It was, however, overhung by a most beautiful pink double hibiscus and might have been regarded as an idyllic spot.

'A bit fresh' was how Eric described his showerbath when the sun was not actually shining and the same might have been said of the loo, which was a splendid little house made of leaf

'... a splendid little house ... approached by a coral causeway'

Siota

and thatch, up on stilts over the sea and approached by a coral causeway from the end of the garden. I liked it; it was cool and airy and commanded an excellent view of approaching and departing shipping. It had a few slight disadvantages. The tide went out and then children played underneath. It was rather a long way from the house and if one was ill, or if it was raining or the middle of the night, or in any combination of these circumstances one sometimes longed for home comforts; it can be very disturbing to a night's sleep to have to look for a torch and then a raincoat and an umbrella and find a causeway after stumbling down ten steps and walking the length of the garden. And on gusty days with a cyclone blowing up, the whole structure swayed alarmingly and the updraught rushed up and one felt as if one were on the end of a more dangerous Blackpool pier. But, all in all, I thought it was a pleasant little house and we promised ourselves to dine out on it for the rest of our lives.

Most of my thoughts about our living and working conditions I felt obliged to keep to myself. By Melanesian standards, we were certainly very comfortable. Our fellow-missionaries were more experienced than we were (and therefore better dug in), and mostly antipodeans, used to a tougher and more self-reliant way of life than urban pommies like us. The deficiencies of the food, though enough to bring me out in a miserably protracted and quite unprecedented crop of boils, were largely the result of our newness and inexperience as island-dwellers, but the first three months were hard to bear. Guests were an embarrassment. Our very first, the diocesan education secretary, arrived one day for a meeting of the Gela education committee. He stayed for fifteen days because of lack of shipping to get him back to his office in Honiara and he must have been pretty sick of corned horse and 777 sandwiches by the time he got away.

I must have expressed in letters to England some of what I suppressed in Melanesia, for an old friend, a London barrister's wife, to whom I wrote in answer to a Christmas card,

Married to Melanesia

explaining that I had married Robinson Crusoe and had not had time to notify everybody, was so horrified by my middle-aged antics that she rushed round the corner to Harrods and despatched us a food parcel. This, of course, had to make its final way to us by diocesan ship and it arrived considerably dishevelled, tins of this and that having broken loose and rolled around the deck. The *pièce de résistance* was an enormous square tin of fancy biscuits which was stoved in and ruined. I wrote a letter of dignified remonstrance to Harrods, expressing surprise at the inadequacy of their packing, and, four months later, we received another tin of crumbs. They made a pleasant base for several trifles.

III

MOTHER, FATHER AND AUNT JANE

I have never – yet – been a vicar's wife, though Eric has been a vicar and he tells me that my initial astonishment and dismay at some features of our life in the Solomons would have been modified if I had been broken in by life in an English vicarage. This may be so, but I find it hard to imagine elsewhere so extreme an expectation that we would be father, mother and Aunt Jane to an entire community as we found at Siota. I had thought I was marrying a theologian who had undertaken a specific academic job – the sort of thing I was familiar with – in however remote a place. Instead, I found myself more in the position of, say, the lady of the manor in a self-contained English village in the eighteenth century with the big house taking its social responsibilities seriously. (I cannot remember whether Sir Roger de Coverley had a wife?) Or perhaps that of an officer – almoner? portress? guest-mistress? – in a medieval abbey with an entire countryside looking to it for help and guidance, while the pattern of daily worship rolled inexorably on and a glimmer of literary culture was preserved against heavy odds.

As far as the people of Gela were concerned, Siota was a mission station. Our activities as a college hardly impinged on them, but the station was the place to which you took your problems and troubles. We sold stamps and posted and received – and if necessary read aloud – people's letters for them. (When I say 'we', I include our students.) If the Government wished to

Married to Melanesia

spread information or a warning to the people – as when we were menaced by the crown of thorns starfish – the mission stations were important means of communication and it was our students who went about the village telling people what they needed to know.

The students ran a community store, which was the shopping centre for the entire neighbourhood. People would run out of petrol for their outboard motors – and apply to Siota. We were not allowed to sell it, but we were usually willing to lend a gallon or two – and it was always repaid.

The wife of an elderly village deacon died in a neighbouring hamlet and the family felt itself sufficiently important to want to bury her in a coffin rather than in the customary mat. They came to us to ask if we had any packing cases and nails. Then to borrow tools. Finally to borrow a spade to dig the grave. Poor old lady; at the end of all these exertions, the coffin with her in it stood in church for the funeral, uneasily supported on two rickety small tables from our sitting room, mutely exhorting us to STOW AWAY FROM BOILERS. Our final good office was to lend the family a sack of rice for the funeral baked meats.

Our medical role I have already mentioned, for this was what dismayed me most after Nonie Connor's departure on leave. Nonie had many adventures. On one occasion, she actually took an old man with no visible relations into her own house to die. She could do nothing for him medically, but she went out and killed one of her chickens and cooked it for him as a treat. He died happy.

All this was immensely time and energy consuming and one often felt impatient to be allowed to get on without distraction and do the job one was qualified to do. But when you are the *only* small pocket of technical civilisation in a wide, if sparsely populated area with poor communications, and when you profess an incarnational religion and believe in a compassionate God, you have to do the best you can for people's needs with what material goods and elementary skills you have.

Siota was perhaps an extreme example; later, after we moved

Mother, Father and Aunt Jane

to Guadalcanal, our responsibilities to the neighbourhood somewhat diminished, though we are still in heavy demand as a taxi service, especially for ladies who are about, as they say, to deliver, which they tend to do at inconvenient hours. But I know of many parts of the Solomons where a mission station is even more remote from Honiara. Our friend, Archdeacon Brock in the Outer Eastern Islands, with his school and his store and his semi-episcopal district to get round in his little ship, is much more isolated than we ever were. But, unlike us, he is one of nature's resourceful, all-purpose missionaries, an English bachelor, retired army-officer, former farmer, former prison-chaplain; and he likes his remote life so much that he proposes to live and die on his outer island, having recently been back to England and liked what he saw there a good deal less.

Things will certainly change with political and educational development in the Solomons, but at this stage the position of the church in society is surprising and very unfamiliar to the newcomer from the secularised West. Almost everywhere, Christianity has taken over an entire community, modifying itself somewhat in the process but replacing the old social structures and customary sanctions with more or less Christian new ones. Partly because of geographical isolation and partly as a result of agreements among Christian missions in the early twentieth century, there has been much less overlapping and competition for converts than in many parts of the world, with the result that some entire islands are not only solidly Christian but solidly Anglican. So it is possible to live – for instance on Gela or Santa Isabel – in the sort of unitary society, speaking culturally and ideologically, that has not existed in England since at least the sixteenth century. Here and there on some islands, though not on all and not on Gela, heathen villages still cling to the old ways but without, one suspects, any great conviction. The whole Protectorate was recently agog with interest at a news story on the local radio of the birth of Siamese twins to a woman in North Malaita and we all eagerly followed

Married to Melanesia

the story for several weeks until it was reported that the babies had died. What interested many people was that the village where the twins were born was still heathen and the father, in fact, was a 'custom' priest. According to custom, the birth had taken place outside the village – in a cave, it was reported – and the father, also according to 'custom', was not permitted to see his offspring for thirty days. Somebody must have gone down to the coast and alerted the nearest small clinic, which happened to be at a Catholic mission station, and one of the Sisters had gone out to see what could be done. It was clearly necessary to take the mother and children down to the clinic with a view to getting them to Honiara and a surgeon as soon as possible, but 'custom' further decreed that the newly delivered mother could not use the normal bush path; if she had done so, no man would ever have been allowed to use it again. So the Christian schoolboys in the mission station were got out by their teacher and priest and they cut a new path for several miles through the bush to the poor woman's cave and she was helped down to the coast where the twins, joined at the abdomen, were said to be doing reasonably well. In the end, one of them succumbed to pneumonia and died; the other one naturally died too. I think the thirty days were up by then and the father did actually see them alive. Many people commented on the quite unnecessary hardship caused to the poor mother by the tyranny of 'custom' and remarked that things would have been even worse for her if there had not been, for instance, some Christian schoolboys around as well as a nursing sister.

Villages like this are unlikely to remain pagan for much longer, but when they are converted it will be as a body because everybody in a village does everything together. One sometimes hears of villages which are waiting to become Christian till their old heathen priest dies; they do not want to hurt the old man's feelings. We even had a student once whose father was a heathen priest. He had wished the boy to follow in the family tradition but realised that times were changing, so he sent him to school and consented to his baptism and encour-

Mother, Father and Aunt Jane

aged him to volunteer for training as a Christian priest. This did not seem to strike anybody as very remarkable or unreasonable. Luke said his father remembered eating human flesh in his youth. It tasted, the old man said, much like pig.

It was the Church which brought to the Solomons the first Western medicine, the arts of reading and writing and – perhaps most important of all – some degree of unity. The existence of seventy-three separate languages in a population of 161,000 (1970 census figures) is evidence of the past extreme isolation of communities, not only one island from another but one village from the next. During the past hundred years, mission ships have done much to break down this isolation. Schools have been started and young people, gathered together from separated communities, have learned to live and communicate with each other. Missionaries and local priests and catechists and teachers have got around. The effect of this in the Anglican area has been to produce a real sense of community within the diocese, rather ahead of a sense of national community, which is only now developing.

'The diocese' has become a familiar enough unit to me over five years in Melanesia, but I remember how odd I found it when I first heard it used. To be told – inaccurately, as it turned out – in a letter from a fellow-missionary when I was collecting linen and equipment in England for our residence in the Solomons and checking on what to buy, that he 'didn't think there was a double bed in the diocese' excited my ribald laughter; but I think I could – almost – write the same sort of thing myself now, and with a straight face. Certainly I was flattered when I was told – not by a bishop, to whom these locutions must come naturally, but by a young Australian electrician – that I had the reputation of being the best cook in the diocese; but I found nothing remarkable in his turn of phrase.

The priest (local or foreign) and the missionary are accorded a respect and importance in this society that I still find embarrassing if occasionally useful. Eric thinks that our total freedom from anxiety about theft is partly attributable to the *mana* of

31

Married to Melanesia

the priest which makes our property tabu, but I believe that the unusual honesty of local society, outside Honiara at any rate, has more to do with it. The Church has been responsible – and still is responsible – for most of the formal education which has been given in the Solomons and this has had the effect of making very many of the people who have been to school – shop assistants, garage hands, policemen, customs officers – curiously filial in their attitude to, at any rate senior missionaries. When I was in the government hospital in Honiara for a few weeks recovering from surgery, I found that the young nurses, of both sexes, were nearly all recent products of diocesan schools. I had never seen them before, but they knew who I was and treated me at once as *ex officio* adviser, lender of a wristwatch, reminder of time, and so on, because I was a senior member of the diocesan family. I do not think they realised at all that my medical ignorance was nearly total; indeed, I got into the habit, after one or two lapses of memory which left me lying unbandaged and exposed while they looked for something they had forgotten at the other end of the hospital, of running my eye over their trolley when they came to do a dressing and saying, off-handedly, 'What about the so-and-so?' – a tactic which one would never dare employ in any hospital where one was not, unofficially, a sort of honorary grandmother. If this adds up to a deplorable paternalism – maternalism? – I can only plead that a determinedly impersonal response to the confiding approach of these young people would be intolerably priggish and downright churlish.

All the same, Eric and I did bring with us to the Solomons all the guilt-feelings of the Western liberal about European paternalism, reinforced in my case by having lived through the anti-colonial revolution in Ghana and become accustomed to plain speaking on the subject from black colleagues and pupils, to say nothing of the newspapers. We also shared – and still share – the insights of our time about the Church, preferring to see it as a body of responsible, adult Christians, each performing his own function, than as a flock of witless sheep

Mother, Father and Aunt Jane

driven about by kindly shepherds. These insights we are quite consciously trying to communicate to our students, the future shepherds and leaders, deliberately rejecting paternalist attitudes towards them and encouraging them in their turn to look for responsible co-operation from the people they will be sent to minister to. But hierarchical attitudes are very deeply ingrained in this society and the priest is going to maintain his social prestige for a long time yet, whatever his own attitude to his function may be. European dominance, on the other hand, will probably suffer a sharp decline and we may well be living through its last decade. Eric's successor will be a Melanesian and it will be interesting to see how much his role will change. Meanwhile, we are conscious that our five years in Melanesia have just lain within the period of the dominant missionary and that we have been – however reluctantly – heirs of that nineteenth-century tradition of power and prestige.

One thing we have always been thankful for as members of this Christian society in the Solomons is the enlightened policy of the Anglican missionary pioneers in these parts. Unlike some other nineteenth-century English missionaries in the Pacific, our own Victorian founding fathers were men of a wide and liberal culture and they did not try to reproduce the *mores* of British *petit bourgeois* society among their converts. They did not suggest that the people should wear clothes, or give up their traditional dances, or work regular hours and practise thrift, or, indeed, change any of their customs except those which were positively inconsistent with a Christian way of life, such as cannibalism. The result is a Christian community singularly free from cant. Sunday morning after church is a favourite time for football matches and our students who go on for further studies in Fiji where they meet other Pacific Islanders are astonished at their Sabbatarianism (and, no doubt, the others are deeply shocked by the Solomon Islanders' laxity). In Tonga, for example, the police are quite capable of arresting people who go on to the beach for a bathing-picnic on Sunday, and I am told that if your wife goes into labour after midnight

Married to Melanesia

on Saturday and you want to take her to hospital in a taxi, you have to begin by asking police permission.

The Church in contemporary Solomon Islands society provides a great many of the occasions for celebration, but the celebrations are traditional and always include 'custom' dancing, which is much enjoyed by all and has certainly not been rejected, as in some other places, by the educated young. I have seen what London or New York would no doubt call 'topless dancers' celebrating the consecration of our new cathedral. Nobody has ever suggested to them that there is anything immoral or improper about the traditional costume of grass skirts, which is what people wear for dancing. It will be a pity – but it may happen – if the vulgarity of tourists makes 'custom' dancing into a titilating spectacle, but, meanwhile, the Church in these parts cannot be accused of prudery or of undue interference in the people's harmless way of life.

IV

DAVID

The Connors employed a houseboy, Dudley, from Boromole, a village which was visible from Siota about a mile away across the Boli Passage, a strip of water which divides the whole island into Big Gela and Small Gela. Siota lies on Small Gela at the end of the Passage; our house faced across the Passage towards Boromole. If one walked round the corner, one could look out over the open sea and catch a distant view of the big island of Malaita. Dudley recruited one of his mates from the village, Cecil, to work for us. (These aristocratic English names, which are very common in the Solomons, derive from the early missionaries of nearly a century ago, when the Melanesian Mission had connections with Eton.)

Dudley was indeed a boy, of about nineteen or twenty. Nonie said that the boy scouts had done a lot for his education and, sure enough, Cecil in turn asked for half a day off to be a boy scout when he came to Siota, where the students ran a troop. We felt that at about forty-five he was a bit past being a scout recruit, but acquiesced.

He was a funny little man with a curious grin which revealed a mouthful of teeth totally blackened by years of chewing betel-nut and tobacco. One would have guessed at sight that he was quite illiterate, but he turned out to be the village church 'reader'. I do not think he had any previous experience of working in a house, which was disconcerting to me – accustomed to a well-organised and experienced African servant – for nothing could be taken for granted. For example, I asked him to clean our bedroom and turned my back for five minutes

Married to Melanesia

to find him pouring buckets of water over everything, apparently under the impression that he was swabbing down a ship's deck. He had, indeed, something of the air of a shipwrecked sailor, as did many of our associates and callers, from the rural dean to our 'member' on the legislative council. This was, I suppose, because of living so much in and out of canoes; I soon found out for myself that in the conditions of Solomon Islands life it was nearly impossible to stay clean and tidy, let alone elegant, and probably began to look shipwrecked myself, but I did not let my clothes get really dirty and I did not stink of tobacco as Cecil did, to my great discomfort in the kitchen.

After a few weeks, he proposed that he should take a holiday; we thankfully agreed, and made it a permanent one. He was succeeded by Bartholomew, a mere boy, who lasted perhaps two months. He was flighty and often missing when needed, though he could usually be found at the end of the jetty, catching fish for himself. He too came from Boromole across the water. Very early one morning, about four o'clock, we were wakened by anguished kitten mewing. We both got up and began to search with our torches for our little cat, Kate, the heroine of the corned beef, who must, we thought, be shut in somewhere, but we found her, perfectly all right and puzzled to see us, in her accustomed hunting ground around the causeway to the loo. Still the crying went on. Finally Eric opened the lid of the dustbin on the back veranda and revealed a small, black kitten, protesting bitterly, which we exhumed from the rubbish and fed. Soon after, it was time to go to church. When I came back, rather ahead of Eric, at about a quarter to seven Bartholomew was in the kitchen and the dustbin loud with renewed cries. 'It's a kitten!' I said. 'How did it get back in there?' Bartholomew was complacent. 'My pussy', said he. He had, it seemed, found it in the bush on some mysterious expedition of his own in the middle of the night and had incarcerated it in our dustbin until such time – the following afternoon – as he should be ready to take it to Boromole in his canoe. To Boromole it did indeed go, but only after a day at

David

large and monopolising my time and attention, keeping it out of the way of the jealous Kate.

Bartholomew's flightiness finished his career as a houseboy. He went off to a feast in a village down the Passage and did not reappear for a week, by which time we had been taken over by David.

David is a citizen of Belaga, that great city, three miles from Siota. With its five hundred inhabitants, it must be the largest of the Gela villages. David has worked at various jobs on two of the Gela mission stations and also in Honiara in a rice mill and a saw mill, so he is a man of the bigger world. He worked for a short time for a woman anthropologist from Holland, whom he liked. I bet he told her some tall stories. He is enterprising, always at the front of the crowd, venturesome and bold. He has been up in a helicopter, which is more than I have. When some visiting geologists were prospecting on Gela by helicopter and came down at Belaga asking questions about places, it was characteristically David who was at the front of the crowd and saying boldly, 'Let me come with you. I'll show you.' He had worked for Eric's predecessor, but I think he found his wife too bossy and the children too troublesome. A previous missionary employer, to whom he had been very loyal, even to the point of letting him get married (he had, naturally, been at the wedding) had been transferred to a distant island. And now he had been sizing up the new warden of Siota and his wife from the safe distance of Belaga, had decided that we would do, and was moving in to take us over.

When he came to us, David was a widower with a little daughter, Margaret, whose mother had died when she was born, about seven years earlier. He continued to live at Belaga and he walked the three miles to Siota every day. We got on well from the beginning. It was already known that we were intending to move the college to Guadalcanal eight or nine months later and I was astonished when David said to me, within a week of his engagement, 'Shall we go?' Go we all did and David has ever since been an essential member of our

Married to Melanesia

household which he treats as his household, referring to 'our car' or 'our sewing machine', and so on. He operates with a stout spirit of independence (he would never dream of addressing me as 'madam' as all my African servants did) and sometimes puts me in mind of the servants in French classical comedy with his outspoken interest in and ready comment on all our concerns, plans, letters, invitations and any conversations held within his hearing. He is intelligent and quick and likes to organise his work in his own way and his own time. This suits me well, as I dislike standing over anybody at work, but I could sometimes wish he required less audience participation in his activities. My own reading and writing are much interrupted by excited cries of 'Mrs Jones! Mrs Jones!' and he likes me to run to the scene and comment. His faults as a worker are so like my own that I have not the face to administer many rebukes. He likes to do three jobs at a time and generally forgets at least one of them half-way through in the unexpected emergencies that arise from the other two; so that everybody present ends by rushing to deal with simulataneously overflowing water tanks, escaping fowls, milk boiling over the stove and a living-room – which they had hoped to sit down in for a mid-morning cup of coffee – with all its chairs on the table or the front lawn. This is so like my own methods and exasperates me so much less than the spectacle of somebody rooted to the spot, waiting for a kettle to boil, that I am resigned to living in an exciting chaos and simply try to protect Eric, who is not, from the worst effects of it.

David is a man who was born twenty years too early. With his quick intelligence and (for a Melanesian) unusually extrovert disposition, he would have gone far if he had been a schoolboy at the present moment of national awakening. But he never went to school at all. He has taught himself to read and write and he speaks and understands English better than some of our newly-arrived students. He has some odd pronunciations which I am told are peculiar to Gela people; he confuses 'p's with 'f's. I am now accustomed to hanging out

David

the washing with 'fegs' and laying the table with 'flates', eating 'fuddings' at 'peasts' and putting 'pish' in the 'pridge'. The one which reduced me to helpless laughter – we were both giggling already in any case – was the occasion when David was helping me to manoeuvre a heavy spring mattress around when we were rearranging the bedroom furniture. It kept springing back on us and knocking us over and finally it penned David in a corner so that he could not get out without climbing over. Laughing aloud, he said, 'Like a fig', which momentarily puzzled me till I realised he felt like an animal confined to what we call in the Solomons (be it cows, hens, or, as in this case, pigs) its fence.

David has a lively linguistic curiosity of a kind which I found very common in Ghana but, to my great disappointment as a teacher, almost entirely absent in Solomon Islands students. He is constantly asking me the meaning of English words he hears on the radio and getting me to write them down. Admittedly, this is partly because, like nearly all the younger people in the Solomons, he is an avid consumer of pop music, sends in his weekly 'request' to the Solomon Islands Broadcasting Service, and listens carefully till he hears it on the air. One of his earliest purchases after we came to Guadalcanal was a transistor radio, which he eventually sent over to Belaga for Margaret and her grandmother, where it was – he improbably reports – wrecked by being struck by a cricket ball flying in through the window. Since then he has had our transistor on a long and increasingly permanent loan. I know he is on his way back to work after breakfast by the approach of pop as he comes down the road. Luckily, the SIBS has a close season for much of the day, except for 'Teachers' Teatime' at ten o'clock in the morning and 'Lunch Date' at noon; these two sessions keep me in touch with rather out of date pop between them.

We are often worried about David's future. Certainly, most Solomon Islanders are essentially peasant farmers and regard work for wages as an interlude in their lives which they expect to spend mainly on the land. But David is a man of such enter-

David being helpful and friendly to the ladies of Minnesota

David

prise and liveliness that we cannot see him sinking contentedly back into the tedium of village life. There is obviously no future for houseboys as such. But most jobs, even here, require some schooling and David has no paper qualifications at all. Except his driving licence. Between us, we have taught him to drive our car and topped the instruction off by a course of professional driving lessons in Honiara on a truck. There have been incidents – as with most learner drivers – such as the occasion when he reversed into a deep ditch on the compound, taking a lump off the corner of the library and doing no good at all to the car, but he has learnt and he has acquired his precious document and he is, with practice, making a good driver. With his conversational powers and lively interest in everything, he would be ideally suited to driving tourists round – if our hoped-for tourist boom comes to anything – and this is how I see him in my mind's eye, helpful and friendly to the flustered matrons from Minnesota and telling them such a tale . . .

V

MOVING

When we came to Siota, we already knew that the diocese of Melanesia had a plan to reorganise the whole pattern of education and training for the various kinds of ministry in the Church. In future, it was intended that the priests should receive their training alongside others: catechists and lay leaders, teachers of religion in schools, perhaps – daring thought – even women, all in one central institution which could also be available for short courses and conferences, refresher courses for the clergy and so on. We hoped that the new institution would be a lively place, open to the world and capable of stimulating the thinking of the local Church at a time when the whole of society is waking up and trying to find the place it wants in the modern world.

That was the vision. St Peter's at Siota in remote isolation was hardly the ideal site for such a renaissance. But the diocese also had St Andrew's Catechist College on the island of Guadalcanal, twenty-three miles west of Honiara, but the nearest available piece of church land to that metropolis; the plan was to unite the two institutions under the name of Bishop Patteson Theological Centre. (Bishop Patteson was the founder-bishop of the diocese, the original Etonian in fact, and a very great Victorian indeed. He was murdered in 1871 on the island of Nukapu as an act of revenge against white men in general, whom the islanders regarded as collectively responsible for the iniquities of the slave-trade in 'labourers' for the sugar plantations of Queensland and Fiji. His memory is still green and he is very much our beloved saint and martyr.)

Moving

Half-way through our year at Siota, Eric and I went across to Honiara for a meeting and we drove out to visit our prospective home at Kohimarama. The name is a Maori word meaning 'place of light'. It was first given to the original school for islanders which Bishop Selwyn, another Victorian giant, established at Auckland in New Zealand. The name moved round the Pacific with the school itself and finished up on Guadalcanal with St Andrew's.

We liked the place at once. It is about a mile inland, on a river, with a magnificent view up to the uninhabited and pathless mountains. The soil was obviously superior to that of Gela. Everything was green and lush and rested the eyes after the glare of the sand and the sea and the coral at Siota. It was also just off the road which runs along the north coast of Guadalcanal in either direction from Honiara, stimulating communication between villages and town and indeed social and economic life generally. In the dryish season in the middle of the year, our small hired car did the twenty-three miles quite happily and negotiated the unbridged rivers – six or seven of them, three quite major – without trouble. We rejoiced at the idea of having a vehicle instead of boats and being within reach of the capital with its shops and post office and hospital. And we were delighted at the prospect of moving our students from their monastic seclusion to within reach of other students, a football league and any cultural life from the wider world that gets as far as the Solomon Islands.

St Andrew's had a dining-hall, one dormitory and two staff houses built in permanent materials – concrete floor, frame walls, iron roof. The rest was 'leaf' – Melanesian buildings in traditional style, home-made from local materials with support posts made from bush trees and walls and roof made from panels of stitched pandanus ('sago-palm') leaves. Leaf houses are pleasant and cool but unsuitable for many purposes. They are always infested with boring insects so that a fine dust rains down all the time and covers everything with a film; they are impossible places to keep books in. Also their life

Married to Melanesia

is short – people reckon five years – and they easily blow down in cyclones. A good many of the St Andrew's leaf buildings were past or at the very end of their useful life and it was planned to replace them as quickly as possible with permanent buildings. There was some money and the diocesan building department had a team of men ready to begin operations.

Eric decided that the move must be made in time for the academic year due to begin in February 1970. The essential new building was a library to house the fairly good collection of books from Siota. This must also allow for expansion and provide a place for the students to sit and work in. A third staff house was also needed, as there were to be three staff families at the start. Some permanent student married quarters were projected, but only two were eventually built. The remaining student families were provided with new leaf houses, put up, on contract, by local villagers. The existing leaf dormitory, classroom and chapel, though very dilapidated, might just last another year and, once we were in residence, our students themselves would be able to build more classrooms.

Eric made two more brief visits of inspection, reported very slow progress, partly because of staff changes and other emergencies in the running-down stages of St Andrew's, and finally decided that we would move over regardless and let the new centre be built round us, since this seemed the only way of getting anything done. We managed to book the landing-craft (ex-Second World War) *Vonu* from the Government, as one might call in a firm of removers at home, and 14 March was designated Moving Day. This would give us a very late start to the academic year, but we felt better a month late than a whole year. As there was not enough room on the *Vonu* for 'olgeta', plus all our individual and corporate possessions, the diocesan ship, the *Baddeley*, would take the women and children across in advance. 'In advance' turned out to mean a fortnight in advance. The students' wives and Nonie Connor and I packed ourselves up a limited ration of luggage and domestic

Moving

gear and food, and the *Baddeley* arrived one sparkling morning at the jetty.

Students rushed into our house to pick up my loads and were sent off with various prepared packages by Eric while I searched for Kate, the cat, a reluctant prospective voyager who had gone missing the moment we got out her basket. The Connors' Timid, the sole survivor of the bachelor brothers, was already on board, patiently sitting in his basket under a chicken-wire lid, but Kate was nowhere to be found and the ship was ready to sail. Finally we found her in the roof space of our house, captured her with difficulty, stuffed her into her basket and a flustered cat, wowling dismally, accompanied an equally flustered warden's wife over the side of the ship on to the deck. I felt a bit like the obstreperous Mrs Noah in the medieval plays, for the ship lost no time in departing and my farewells were cut short. I have never seen Siota again.

We had a smooth voyage of four or five hours, with twenty or thirty small children behaving well, eating lumps of 'pudding' and apparently giving no concern to their mothers about falling overboard; everybody is used to journeys by sea. Kate continued to wowl, so I had her out of the basket. She walked about the cabin floor and ended up on my lap, where she was seasick. We were making for the point on the Guadalcanal coast nearest to Kohimarama. We had to look out for a river-mouth with the road coming close to the shore and a small, sandy beach. The landmark for the beach was a tin-roofed Chinese-owned store standing by the road immediately opposite (and subsequently known to us English as Harrods and to our Australian colleagues as David Jones, after the big department store in Sydney). All this was sighted, the anchor was dropped, the ship's boat launched and we and our babies and cats jumped overboard in turns and were paddled ashore, where Jim Blades, our new Australian colleague who had already moved in from another Gudalcanal station, awaited us. He had laid on a tractor and trailer from the nearby plantation at Tanaemba to take our gear up the hill to Kohimarama. I waited to check my things

Married to Melanesia

from the hold and in due course everything came ashore except one large suitcase which contained all my clothes and household linen. The crew searched again – but it had clearly been left behind in the anxiety about the cat.

So I arrived at Kohimarama in what I stood up in. One does not travel on diocesan ships in one's best and the cat had, in any case, been sick over the dress, such as it was. Neither Nonie Connor's nor Elizabeth Blades's clothes would fit me, but Elizabeth was able to supply a nightdress which did not, to the unsophisticated eye, look too unlike street costume (there were no streets anyhow) and some sheets and towels and thus I started my career on Guadalcanal.

The *Baddeley* sailed off, taking a radio message asking Eric to send my clothes to Honiara if opportunity offered, a message which gave much innocent pleasure to many who overheard it on their wireless sets, and the Bladeses explained that in any case we were cut off by road from Honiara after recent rains which had flooded the rivers. They had a car of their own, but it was not actually at Kohimarama having been abandoned at the Tanaemba Plantation after their last trip to town during which the bridge over the Tanaemba River had fallen down. I, who had had visions of collecting the Mini-Moke we had ordered three months earlier and meeting the landing craft with this, had to revise my plans.

At Kohimarama, further shocks awaited us. The students' leaf houses were not finished and neither was ours. Nonie and one-year-old Sean Connor and I were able to move into the empty staff house and the Melanesian Brothers, our neighbours, of whom more later, generously lent the student families their own 'bush houses' down by the river. We made sure that everybody had a roof of some sort over their heads and something to eat and we all went to bed.

The next fortnight scarcely bears recollection. We lost our frightened cats and spent hours in the heat and the sun looking for them. We were worried about the women, though I realise now that they were far more capable of looking after themselves

Moving

without their husbands or their possessions than we were. We were missing what home comforts we had had at Siota, notably our kerosene-operated refrigerators, without which it is impossible to keep anything fresh for half a day, and I was missing my clothes. To make matters worse, Nonie slashed her hand while putting up a clothes-line and the wound turned alarmingly sceptic. She ran a high temperature and insisted that she would have to be got to hospital – and we knew we could rely on her medical judgement. The only vehicle, the Bladeses' car, could not be got to Honiara, but we did manage to send a message along the coast and then by radio to the hospital, which sent out a Land-Rover to cross the rivers and pick her up at our road end. Sean was thus deprived of both his parents as well as being in a strange place and this naturally increased our problems.

I decided to try to set up house somehow before the men arrived and borrowed a couple of old mattresses which I put on the floor, some shelving which seemed to be going spare till the library arrived and which served me for all purposes, a kitchen table and a few steel chairs from a classroom. I also acquired a Primus stove and with this meagre equipment and a few old boxes moved in the day the builders connected the plumbing with a temporary pipe from the water tank at the Connors' house. Water, at this stage, was no problem; torrential rain was falling, we were living in a sea of mud and our road was cut, but the tanks were overflowing.

March 14th, however, was sunny and hot. The *Vonu*, I knew, had been hired for the day and was due at Siota at first light. The men intended to load her as quickly as possible and hoped to sail by mid-morning and arrive at our beach any time after 1 p.m. I had no great confidence in this schedule, but at 1.30 I took a novel and made my way down to the beach, where I spent a pleasant literary afternoon under a coconut palm. At four o'clock, the horizon was still empty and I decided to walk the mile home to listen to the radio in case there was a message. Outside the house, I found the Dean of

Married to Melanesia

Honiara's intrepid Volkswagen which had actually forded the rivers, the Dean himself and a VIP from the Canadian Church who had contrived to break a journey in Honiara specially to come and see the Kohimarama Centre which the Canadians were thinking of supplying with a member of staff. Being an English lady – though my only dress did not look very convincing by now – and knowing that this was the divinely appointed hour for tea, I welcomed these dignitaries into the house, offered them boxes to sit on, lit the Primus stove and got out the plastic mugs and generally tried to behave like the warden's wife. The Canadians, it seemed, were offering us their man on the sole condition that the diocese housed him, so I said yes, he could have a house like ours in due course. The North American looked round and commented that it was a bit rough but would, no doubt, be all right when it had plumbing, a water supply, cooking equipment, a fridge and some furniture. No air conditioning, he said thoughtfully, but perhaps that would come?

There was nothing on the radio about a delayed *Vonu* so I thought I had better return to the beach and the visitors offered to drive me down. By now it was half past five and the sun was beginning to set – but, sure enough, there was a speck on the horizon which eventually turned into the shape of a landing-craft. At this point the Canadian, showing great consideration and common sense, suddenly said, 'Well, I'm sure your husband won't want to see me at this moment. Thank you for your hospitality, Mrs Jones, and goodbye.' With this he and the dean got into the Volkswagen and set off for Honiara and, one hoped, a good dinner at the Bishop's.

The *Vonu* ploughed into the beach, ground over the sand and shingle and lowered its end like a tipper-lorry; the men jumped out and waded ashore to be greeted, by this time, by quite a crowd of wives and children and Brothers and the tractor and trailer. George Connor had to be told that Nonie was in hospital, but while we were deciding how to get him there, she suddenly turned up, having discharged herself and

Moving

set out to walk the twenty-five miles home. Luckily, she had been given several lifts.

The main thing now was to get the *Vonu* unloaded and to send it home to Honiara before the Government could charge us another day's hire, so, as night fell, everything was tossed ashore on to the beach – furniture, pots and pans, refrigerators, blackboards, crates of library books, the altar from the church, several families of domestic fowl in their cages, the pig, sacks of kumara and rice and flour and everybody's *lares* and *penates*. I did not see much of this as I was sent off with the first load to take charge of the chickens and get them fed and watered and settled before darkness made this impossible. I returned with electric torches. The tractor had no lights, but as much as possible was heaped on to the trailer and the driver made his way, time and again, clutching a torch, up to Kohimarama with the stuff. Part of the way was a public road but we do not often see a policeman and nobody objected. Taking turns to eat, the men worked till two o'clock in the morning, which gave them a nineteen-hour day with a sea voyage in the broiling sun in the middle of it. They had spent five hours loading the *Vonu*, which had to be packed like a suitcase, using all the corners, till there was scarcely space to stand up. It was lucky that the sea was very calm that day; a few waves and everything would have been overboard. The unloading only took half an hour and the ship sailed off into the gathering gloom leaving us with all the college's stuff plus everybody's personal possessions in a confused heap on a beach by a public road and just opposite 'Harrods' which is very much a neighbourhood centre, the place where the lads of the district gather together, when they have any money, to smoke their tobacco and consume – technically off the premises – the beer which the Chinaman sells. We simply could not get everything moved that night and it says much for the honesty of Solomon Islanders that nothing whatever was lost or stolen in the whole gigantic move. There was a moment, some weeks later, when I thought we had lost something. We had been to Fiji to a conference the

49

Everything came ashore

Moving

January before we moved and had taken the chance, coming home by air, of buying our allowance of duty-free liquor and tobacco. Lent had immediately supervened; we gave up these indulgences and packed our stocks away in a carton, which I naïvely labelled (I was, necessarily, labelling everything) JONES, DRINKS, CIGARETTES. After Easter, I remembered its existence, but neither of us had seen the carton in the unloading and distribution so we sadly concluded that it had been among the things left on the beach and had, not surprisingly, disappeared. Not a bit of it. Weeks later, I found it among a lot of old boxes in our outside store, quite undamaged by its experiences. We were able to have a party to celebrate our reunion with our drinks.

But on that first night it was all we could do to crawl on to our mattresses on the floor and listen with some anxiety – for nothing much was under cover – to the rain starting.

VI

NEW HOME

Our new house has a number of advantages over the Siota cricket pavilion, notably the kitchen. This, like the house, is rather too small and boxlike for our manner of life, but it contains a gas cooker which has wrought a great domestic transformation, making possible everything from a casual cup of tea in a hurry to the regular baking of bread at home. We came nearer to resigning over the cooking facilities for the new house than we ever have over anything else with the sole exception of the principle that there must be academic standards. The Bishop had fancied a solid-fuel burning stove (i.e. a Moloch, burning great lumps of wood from the bush) in a tropical kitchen eight feet by twelve and nine feet high; he seemed rather put out when we expressed our dismay at the prospect of smoke, heat and sheer hard labour, to say nothing of the endless anxiety about scrounging wood to burn. We won this round, but we did have to wait several months for the gas stove to come from Australia; I was by then well accustomed to camp cookery anyhow and the stove was worth waiting for.

The kitchen was fitted up under my eye after we had moved in. The diocesan carpenters have an obsession with meat safes which they have learnt to make very well (the meat safe seems to be to the tyro carpenter much what the dirndl skirt is to the schoolgirl dressmaker) and found it hard to believe that I did not want a meat safe at all, but would like cupboards. In the end, we reached a compromise. My kitchen was fitted up from floor to ceiling with open shelves and has ever since looked

Kohimarama

Married to Melanesia

like a village shop, with twenty tins of meat in a row, flanked by sixty tins of sardines, Pussy's 'Tucker Box', condensed milk, instant coffee, pounds and pounds of tea and many other things, all imported by the carton from Australia or even England. It is this shameless display of wealth (I *do* wish I could have had cupboards with their modest doors) far more than my aunt's silver tea service deployed on what passes for the sideboard, which makes me feel obscenely rich in a poor country, and it speaks volumes for the honesty of Solomon Islanders that we can go not merely out but away for weeks at a time without locking it all up or even locking the house. My aunt's silver tea service always survived my many Ghana burglaries, but tins of meat are another thing.

I like my kitchen here. It is, oddly enough, the coolest room in the house, being shaded by an enormous mango tree which has rarely produced a mango for human consumption (the fruit bats always get them first) but earns its living in many other ways. It is host to a fascinating collection of epiphytes, including tree-orchids, and I have planted lilies in its shade. Beyond it is our pleasantest view, Mount Popoki, about 2,000 feet high, conical at the top (it is said to be a 'chimney' from the neighbouring volcano of Savo Island, about which we once had a scare, but it came to nothing; somebody had set up their seismological instruments over a growing banana-root), and beautiful in every light. Mount Popoki is a sure index of approaching rain and when the clouds lie low and heavy on it, it reminds me of my Westmorland home. But I think I have enjoyed it most in clear weather at sunset, and especially at moonset at times just after the full of the moon when I have been in the kitchen in the very early morning, making a pot of tea on the precious gas stove by candlelight and watching the moon go down, inch by inch, over 'our' mountain in the before-dawn cool.

The rest of the house consists of an L-shaped living room, a fair-sized bedroom and a small spare bedroom which doubles as my study (Eric has his office elsewhere). There is a minute

New Home

shower-room and a WC. This last might be thought an improvement on the Siota arrangements and so it normally is, but during our first two years at Kohimarama we often looked back on the sea and its cleansing power with some regret. The shower-room is a distinct come-down from the spacious and lordly bathroom of the Siota house, uncertain as the water supply was there. Perhaps it is a feature of middle-age, but I do not take kindly to cold showers and I dislike barking my ankles on rough concrete and, all in all, I think one of my highest domestic ambitions is to be mistress of a proper bathroom with hot water in taps and *no concrete visible* (or, indeed, palpable).

The house suffers from being a prototype, invented and constructed by the diocesan building department who were learning as they went on. They are obviously improving, building by building, and their present efforts are very creditable, but ours was one of their first houses. The major and irremediable error was to build in solid concrete. As there is no veranda and precious little overhang from the roof, the walls stand unshaded and act like night-storage heaters, soaking up the sun's heat all day and continuing to diffuse it long after dark. A layer of insulation under the corrugated iron roof had been planned but was forgotten, so we initially had quite an oven. Eric made the builders come back and crawl about in the roof space (a very hot and horrid job) putting in the insulation and we afterwards employed a villager to rig us up a 'leaf' awning along the sunniest side of the house. This made an enormous difference to the temperature and has also given our uncompromising concrete box a pleasantly cottage look, especially since plants have been persuaded to grow up the support posts. The first little earthquake produced a few ominous cracks in the walls and also split into two neat halves the porcelain WC cistern, wasting a lot of our precious water before we detected the catastrophe, but its plastic replacement seems to be holding up in spite of more earth tremors and a general tendency for the house to slip down the hill.

Married to Melanesia

Water, indeed, has been one of our major problems at Kohimarama. When we arrived our only source was rain water, fed into concrete tanks from the roofs of all the permanent buildings. Each staff house had its own tank. Tanks at the library, dining-hall and the one permanent dormitory provided drinking water, but not much beyond that, for the students and student families. The students, who had had showers at Siota and similar sanitary arrangements to ours over the sea, were condemned to using pit latrines and bathing in the river until such time – it worked out at two years after all the delays – as we could improve the water-supply and build proper ablution blocks for men and women.

During the rainy season all the tanks overflowed all the time and we rejoiced, in spite of the mud and the frequently closed road. But there is a comparatively dry season which lasts for six months and we had some anxious times during two of these. Praying for rain seems a reasonable thing to do in any Christian – indeed any religious – society which lives near enough the earth to feel cause and effect with some immediacy. Droughts – in fact far worse droughts than any we ever have here in the Solomons – were no new experience for me after years in Africa, nor were prayers for rain. I remember one desperate occasion in Accra when a large urban community practically ran out of water altogether and was being supplied from ships in the harbour. It was in the middle of the dry season and the skies were like brass. The Christians (of all sorts) and the Moslems and the *wolomei* (traditional 'fetish' priests) all betook themselves to prayer but everybody seemed somewhat startled by a tremendous storm which broke on that very day and was resumed after nightfall. I had every vessel in the house out collecting water – the taps had been dry for days – and have vivid recollections of taking an immodest shower-bath and washing my hair under what deluged down – slightly dusty – from the eaves, embarrassingly but only fitfully illuminated from time to time by great flashes of lightning. Our experiences at Kohimarama have never been so absolute

New Home

as this; the river has never run dry. But we have often prayed for rain and never with more spectacular success than one even-song at Siota when the student-officiant, one John Mealue, had hardly opened his mouth – under, it may be said, a perfectly clear sky – and uttered the staid prayer-book prayer, when the heavens opened and we literally waded the hundred yards back to the house from the church. Naturally, nobody had brought an umbrella. John acquired quite a reputation as a rainmaker as a result of this triumph and we were often tempted to put him on as officiant in subsequent emergencies.

Unfortunately, at Kohimarama, prayer proved by no means enough and it was clear that action was required. Our own tank was slowly built from concrete, ring by painful ring, after the house was finished and its completion coincided with the onset of the dry season. We had been managing while the rains lasted with an empty 44-gallon oil drum catching water from the roof. It was frustrating to see the splendid new tank, capable of holding 4,000 gallons, standing dry, week after week, while we humped water up from the river. The procedure was to load the old oil drum on to the back of the little Japanese pick-up we had bought, drive it three-quarters of a mile to the nearest point we could get to the spring in the river and fill it, bucket by bucketful. We lost a fair amount jolting back home over uneven ground and the drum was too heavy to lift off the truck, so there was more bucket work required and a great complication of finding empty vessels. When we had it at home, the water was too precious to waste and we took to bathing, like everyone else, in the river. River bathing on a hot holiday afternoon is pleasant enough, but taking one's daily bath, amid a busy programme, in this way is a downright nuisance. It cannot be done after dark, or, indeed, at dusk when the mosquitoes are intolerable. One is always in a hurry and I always found that the sweat induced by half a mile's brisk walk up a steep hill, clambering over stones, was enough to neutralise the effect of the bath. Still, we were grateful that the river existed and never ran dry and even provided

Married to Melanesia

us with a constantly flowing fresh spring of pure drinking water.

The students and student families had far longer to put up with these conditions than we had. After the first six months, once we got our water tanks full, we were able, with careful management, to keep our staff houses reasonably well supplied. But we could not give the whole community decent facilities until a well was dug. People told us – with perfect truth – that Solomon Islanders are used to bathing in rivers, or the sea, and do not mind, but it seemed to us that our daily programme is so much fuller and so much more is expected of our students than of villagers, that the primitive arrangements were, at least, inconvenient. I always felt sorry for football teams returning from Honiara after dark in urgent need of a bath and with no recourse but the dark and stony river. A mild outbreak of dysentery then made us fear worse things than mere inconvenience and discomfort.

We took advice from the Geological Survey about wells soon after our arrival at Kohimarama and after due deliberation they started to try to find water for us. They said it should be easy with the river close by. There were many delays – the road would be closed or a senior officer would go on leave or the papers be mislaid or becalmed in an in-tray – but men did come and go and finally, after many months, it was established that there was no water in the place where they had been boring. They suggested another possible spot and went away. We were – as so often happens – on our own. Eric, mildly regretting that civil engineering had been no part of what they had taught him at Oxford, found a friendly Australian in Honiara who offered remote-control advice and he started a do-it-yourself dig with volunteer student labour. By now it was the short August vacation of 1971, eighteen months after the move. Concrete cylinders were bought from the Public Works Department and gradually transported (by ourselves, of course) from Honiara and trundled to the site as a lining. At nine feet, water began seeping in; the site was right. The expert said from afar

New Home

that it would be necessary to go down fifteen more feet, so the men went on digging with their primitive equipment, standing in mud and baling out as they went. Eric aged visibly, not so much from the physical strain of working in the unshaded blaze of the noonday tropical sun – he was not doing much of the physical labour anyway – as from sheer anxiety about the danger of the whole operation, especially one dreadful day when one of the concrete cylinders crashed from a broken rope into the bottom of the well; luckily, there was nobody standing in it at the time to be killed. At nineteen feet, he called a halt. The well was five feet shallower than the experts recommended, but it has proved adequate and has supplied the whole station with enough water all the year round. We have a pump worked by a diesel engine – we toyed for a time with the idea of a windmill – which the students maintain beautifully, and we have a large tank at the highest point of the compound, raised up on stilts. And, two years after our arrival, everybody finally had showers and WCs.

A generator had been installed for the catechist college a few months before our arrival, so we have always had the customary evening's (six to half past ten) electricity supply, proper light being essential for a decent standard of study. We also have an hour of generator in the early morning from half past five, to enable the community to get up and have its morning prayers in the light. I have an electric kettle, an iron and a mixer and Eric has a shaver. There is also an electric fan, which is a lifesaver during the still, hot, humid evenings. I often have the impression that we are standing at the ready, morning and evening, with an appliance in each hand, waiting for the power to come on. Certainly, when some uncovenanted period of electricity happens at an unusual time, I fly round the house looking for ways of capitalising it; at the very least there is always the fan.

More often, it is a breakdown that happens, not a bonanza, and for some reason it usually happens to add to the miseries of the hot, wet season. We returned from our mid-contract

Married to Melanesia

leave in Australia the day after the end of a cyclone in January 1972, to find our road out from Honiara impassable and likely to be so for several weeks. The Bishop sent us home along the coast in the *Southern Cross*. When we got to Kohimarama, we were thankful to find most of the buildings still standing; only a few kitchens, our temporary tutorial rooms (we had new, permanent ones by then) and our garage had been blown away. But our colleagues said the generator was out of action, thought to have been struck by lightning since the trouble had started in the middle of a violent thunderstorm. We waited till the road became precariously open and then brought out a Chinese electrician from Honiara. He examined the generator, but eventually gave up, saying that nobody could sort it out without the manufacturer's handbook and diagrams. We knew that we had not been trusted with these; they had been taken back to the diocesan workshops at Taroaniara on Gela lest any amateur should be tempted to interfere. (This is understandable. That same year, the headmaster of a diocesan school in the New Hebrides had been fatally electrocuted in the course of his handyman activities.) So we sent a radio message to Taroaniara asking for the book. They replied that they could not find it. Perhaps Philip, the chief electrician, who was with the Bishop on the *Southern Cross* touring the mission stations of the New Hebrides and the Banks Islands, had it with him. We sent a cable to Philip who radioed a reply that it was in the top drawer of his desk. Taroaniara said it was not. Weeks slipped by and we got the academic and domestic life organised on a system of oil-lamps and no-iron and doing everything possible by daylight. In the end, the *Southern Cross* returned and Philip came out in person, diagnosed something fairly trivial (this was a relief; we had envisaged further months of waiting for a new part from Japan) and set it right. Illumination! Power! The evening fan!

This was the longest breakdown I have known, but by no means the longest on record. This kind of hazard, combined with the fact that we are responsible (the students do the work

New Home

on a rota system) for the daily maintenance and switching on and off of the generator, makes one very conscious of the sources of our domestic conveniences and comforts. If the lights begin to flicker, or an unusual note is heard in the generator, we are soon plunged into darkness while an anxious group gathers about the patient in the generator house with an electric torch, feeling its pulse and taking its temperature; we cannot afford to neglect any warning signals.

Do-it-yourself is certainly our way of life. When the rains have washed away yet again the three-quarters of a mile of road which we are responsible for, it is the students and the academic staff who are out with the truck, gathering stones from the river and coral from the beach and navvying without benefit of machinery under the blazing sun. Three afternoons a week and Saturday mornings have to be devoted to all the hot and laborious ploys by which our precarious island of material civilisation is kept in working order.

As a result, we do have a modest degree of comfort and convenience, but if there is one thing more than another that I look forward to on our return to England it is not being personally responsible for the town's water supply and the maintenance of the district's roads and bridges. I hope I shall, as an English housewife, bear with fortitude the results of wars and strikes and the running down of civilisation generally; I daresay our island experiences may have made us more ingenious at managing under difficulties. As long as they do not expect us to mend it, whatever it is . . .

VII

STUDENTS

I have said so much about the problems and labours of keeping body and soul together and the plant working adequately that it may well be wondered if the students ever have any time to study, or we to teach, or any of us to get down to some serious reading. And this was precisely the question that presented itself to us when we arrived in the Solomon Islands. It was clear that the general educational level was well below what I had been used to in West Africa and some of the reasons were not far to seek. It was not only at Siota and Kohimarama that so much time was spent on food production, building and maintenance. The schools were run – they had to be, for sheer lack of money – on the same principle. Schoolboys built their own classrooms and dormitories and grew their own food. I remember trying to explain to a class at Kohimarama how butter is made (we were reading something about witchcraft beliefs in seventeenth-century Europe which happened to mention the superstitions about butter-making) only to find them nodding their heads sagely. Half of them, it turned out, had actually *made* butter, which was more than I had. They had had an enthusiastic headmaster at their senior primary school, where they kept cows, and he had tried everything once. All this was admirable, but it did not leave enough time for what is usually understood by school education.

In 1969, only one secondary school in the country went as far as form five. The highest peak of academic achievement possible in the Solomons was the Cambridge Overseas School Certificate; about fifteen students succeeded in getting one that

62

Students

year. External examinations and the standards of the outside world are not all, but they do regulate admission to universities and other professional training courses. Any country aspiring to reasonable modern standards of education and social welfare in the twentieth century must have qualified people to man its services and nobody wants to be for ever dependent on foreigners. By 1969 the Solomon Islands people were beginning to voice their aspirations and Eric's commission to upgrade the training of the clergy was part of the Church's response to this newly-felt need.

But we had to start where we found the students and go on doing what we could with men who were by no means prepared by their previous schooling to undertake any tertiary education. Both at Siota and at Kohimarama we have had two main types of student. Some have come straight from school at the age of nineteen or so. Others have been older, often married and with a young family. These have done various jobs; some have been teachers, some clerks in government departments, a number have worked for the Church as catechists, and we have always had a sprinkling of ex-policemen. Many of the younger ones have had two years of secondary education (most secondary education has stopped at this point even until now). One or two of the older ones have had only three years in school altogether; these have been unusually intelligent and self-educated or they would never have been able to begin on our course. We have to work in English because there are no books for serious study in either pidgin or any of the seventy-three languages spoken in the Solomons – many of them by fewer than 1,000 people – and this is a great difficulty for many of our students but one we can see no way round. It has meant that an entrance examination has had to be set for candidates for admission mainly in order to test whether they understand English well enough to be able to make anything of our courses.

The entrance exam started off one of the first battles Eric fought. The previous system of choosing men for the Church's

Married to Melanesia

ministry had never been able to demand very much in the way of intellectual achievement or even potential. Eric proposed to set up academic standards at two levels, validated by external assessment and requiring serious study and hard work. At the end of our first year we were obliged to send away two or three students (still fairly near the beginning of their course) who quite plainly could not keep up and who would not have been admitted in the first place if there had been any sifting process. They were all good men, as it happened, but it was cruelty to subject them to studies with which they could not begin to cope. Previous dismissals from Siota had all been on grounds of moral delinquency, so the new policy was hard to take and there were those who hinted that it was flying in the face of the Holy Ghost and that education by a process of spiritual osmosis with no intellectual rigours at all was the only decent and devout thing for a Church to do, especially in the South Pacific. Eric and I both felt strongly that it was insulting to Solomon Islanders to imply that they were incapable of thinking for themselves or reaching an acceptable level, by world standards, of competence in their work; the alternative seemed, only too plainly, an ignorant and superstitious clergy unworthy of a people who want to be part of the bigger world. The battle for standards was fought and won; it will not have to be fought again because the new young men who have been educated under the new system will themselves defend the standards.

Meanwhile we got on with teaching and here I felt I was on familiar ground. However useless I might be at the standard ploys of the missionary wife, I had years of experience behind me as a teacher in a foreign background and culture. I had, of course, forgotten about male chauvinism. Admittedly, the students were polite and I *was* the warden's wife, so nobody actually came out with anything like the famous *obiter dictum* of one of my early West African pupils: 'Madam, in *my* country, we men are not accustomed to being abused by a woman.' But the Siota students were all men and they were all candidates for the priesthood and it is quite likely that they

Students

regarded the mere fact of my teaching them as a near-breach of tabu. Also they did not much like being stirred up to think even by Eric who, as well as being a man, carried a certain *mana* as a priest and as warden of the college. So we had many a struggle, but I have persisted, teaching at various times English, history, theology and the Bible; with the passage of time I have become gradually accepted, perhaps making easier the innovation, in our final year, of women students and a woman member of the regular staff. I have learnt many new things myself, especially about Pacific history, and also things about the uses and possible abuses of the English language previously undreamed of in fifteen years of teaching it in Africa. I have also got to know the students themselves far, far better than I could ever have hoped to do simply as the warden's wife.

One of my early ploys was a series of drama groups. It seemed desirable to try to loosen the students up (they struck me, compared with Africans if not with Englishmen, as unnecessarily inhibited), accustom them to speaking audibly and confidently, and also make them use their imaginations. For material we fell back, as we always do, on the Bible. It has many advantages; everybody has a copy, the contents are fairly familiar and it is full of good stories. Also – very important in our early days – it is well known to be 'religious' and seemed related to the students' vocation. Without the Bible, I doubt if we should have been able to sell the 'childish' and quite unclerical idea of improvised play-acting – and in study time too – to the Siota students at all, but sell it we did and soon we had groups all over the beach enacting the adventures of Daniel, Elijah, David and other sanctified characters, with clusters of curious wives and children watching them and making them even more self-conscious.

This first lot almost certainly thought Mrs Jones was some sort of lunatic who could not know what was appropriate to the gravity of an embryo priest, but they humoured me and some of them enjoyed themselves and most of them learnea

Married to Melanesia

a little bit of human psychology from having to improvise dialogue and try to imagine how Elijah or the widow-woman or Jezebel must have felt at the crises of the story. Until one encounters a non-literary culture, one simply does not realise how dependent we Westerners are on fiction and drama – from the adventures of Noddy to the works of Shakespeare – for vicarious experience. I think I have some notion of how it might feel to commit a murder, but it has often struck me that the Melanesians would actually need to do the deed in order to know, not having the experience of Macbeth to go on. So the drama sessions have often turned into exercises of the imagination with me bullying my actors into thinking 'How would I feel if . . . ?' and doing a good deal of demonstration ham-acting myself, I hope they became better priests as a result and I think they probably did.

When we moved to Kohimarama, we had a new first year for whom the syllabus was whatever we said it was and drama became an accepted element. Since then, our first term has always culminated in a made-up, unscripted Bible play, often in pidgin, sometimes in English, sometimes in a mixture as when Joseph and his brethren spoke pidgin and the Egyptians English. We do these plays out of doors over an enormous 'stage' with people tramping about, supposedly over hundreds of miles, often out of earshot of whole sections of the audience, which is also generally pretty mobile and largely juvenile. Terrible scenes break out in the audience if there is any violence on stage (naturally, there usually is) with inconsolable small children being led away because 'daddy' has been killed. Costumes and props are very important elements. Certain tablecloths and furnishings from our house are in great demand, but the students can kit out desert nomads, sheep, cattle, camels, kings, queens, prophets – anything you like – to their own satisfaction with the aid of empty sacks, parts of the coconut tree (especially the fronds and the coarse, untidy 'matting' stuff), trailing vines, hibiscus and frangapani flowers and whatever grows about the place. The nicest thing they ever made, I

Students

thought, was a 'ram' to be caught in a thicket and offered as a sacrifice instead of Isaac. It was a sort of hobby-horse with a rather pig-like head and an interesting look on its face (we do not have sheep here, so nobody knows what they look like or sound like; the student managing it from behind a bush mewed like a cat when told to bleat). I should have liked to keep it but it went up in sacrificial smoke, a burnt-offering to the Lord. Fire, next to costumes, seems to be the other *sine qua non* of our dramas. Abraham's sacrifice, Abel's sacrifice, fire from heaven on Mount Carmel – it does not matter what – but a play without fire is a poor thing. Elijah cheated; he poured some kerosene on the sacrificial site when the audience (or for that matter the priests of Baal) were not looking. People here think nothing of making fire, in the absence of matches, by rubbing two sticks together and I was pleased to see that this was just what Abel did before Cain struck the fatal blow.

It is always real fire, never a let's-pretend one, and this child-like realism is characteristic of all our dramas. If Joseph is to be thrown by his brothers into a hole, a hole is carefully dug in the 'stage' in readiness. I have often wondered how our students would present *Hamlet*'s gravediggers' scene. Or the shipwreck in *The Tempest*? The people in the play, on the other hand, tend to behave like contemporaries. Potipher, in the Joseph story, was a caricature – unconscious I am almost sure – of a certain kind of bourgeois European. The wandering Midianites brought the enslaved Joseph to Potipher's house for sale like some wood-carver hawking his curios round the European civil servants on one of the Honiara ridges, and Potipher came in and said, rather anxiously, to his wife, 'There are some people at the door, my dear. Do we want any slaves?' The purchase price was at length paid out (in Australian currency) from an old plastic handbag which I had thrown away and the whole Potipher episode continued on the same humdrum level with not the faintest hint of the langorous and bored harems of the mysterious East.

For four years I did all the English teaching that could be

Married to Melanesia

fitted into a rather tightly-packed curriculum, regretting all the time that it was not possible to give an intensive crash course to supply the absence of five years at secondary level. I did what I could, concentrating on improving reading and comprehension skills because these were the tools the students most needed in their other studies, and making up most of my own material. I came to the conclusion that the biggest hindrance to acquiring a competent use of English was the existence of pidgin, which everybody has to use as the only *lingua franca* of the region for everyday purposes. Eric and I began by refusing to learn or use it (we were helped by the fact that David was able and willing to talk to us in English and my prejudices were reinforced by the recollection that in West Africa an educated man would be insulted if you addressed him in West African pidgin). This, however, was a mistake as the use of pidgin is on the increase – for example on the radio – and it is, as spoken by habitués, an expressive language, if a bit of a blunt instrument. Admiring a little girl's dress recently, I asked her father, a student, how to say properly in pidgin, 'What a pretty dress!' and was depressed by the reply (I forbear to reproduce the 'accepted' spelling),'Calico good too much.' Shades of meaning simply do not exist in pidgin and probably there is no great richness of such things in the vernaculars; this makes me feel that the Solomon Islanders are inevitably culturally and perhaps emotionally deprived. Not everybody would agree with me, but I strongly suspect that one does not experience distinctions for which one has no language. For example, there seems to be no way of distinguishing concepts such as 'furious', 'resentful', 'irritated', 'bad-tempered' – they all come out as 'cross'; 'sad', 'melancholy', 'depressed', 'unhappy', 'miserable', 'frustrated' – all come out as 'sorry'. This limits self-expression and is also a serious impediment for the readers of ordinary English books, which all our students must become if they are to succeed in their studies. However, pidgin is now being encouraged. The drama groups use it, students practising preaching sermons use it, and there is, I understand, a certain interplay between pidgin,

Students

English and Greek in attempts, at a fairly advanced level, to come at the meaning of the New Testament and especially to make experiments in translation which are very much needed. All this is certainly to the good as the students will have to use pidgin in their future ministry, but it does increase the hazards for anybody trying to teach English.

We make all sorts of efforts, presumably unnecessary in theological colleges in other parts of the world, to supply deficiencies in basic education and to fill up the enormous gaps in our students' general knowledge. In a country without a newspaper, it is hard to whip up as much interest as one would like in current events, but we press on hopefully with courses called 'World and Community', explaining about geography and economics and recent history, analysing government reports and development plans, seizing on visitors and getting them to talk about the places and situations they have come from. Travellers' tales from among their own number are, however, what make the greatest impact on our students. Every year a few have gone on to Fiji to read for a degree and one senses from their letters their bewilderment and awe at the sight of a town the size of Suva with its cosmopolitan population, though they are quick to settle down and enjoy it. One year, Ellison, one of our brightest, had the good luck to be sent to a 'music workshop' in Suva because he had shown some musical talent as a composer. What he had written was some guitar songs in pidgin which he had devised for the Sunday school children who were doing a Christmas play. An American professor of 'ethno-musicology' visiting the workshop was attracted by the songs and by his eager intelligence and she arranged a scholarship for him on a short course at the University of Hawaii if his fare could be found. Found it was, with the aid of the Government, and off Ellison went with his guitar and his tapes and a little newly-imparted knowledge of musical notation, on a plane to Honolulu. He was already on the point of explosion when he left – but the letters that came back! Student accommodation in skyscrapers with himself on

Married to Melanesia

the fourteenth floor! Machines for dispensing coffee! Electric washing machines for the student laundry! Lifts! (He naturally called them elevators.)

But on the whole the Solomons people are not bamboozled by the technology of the modern world and are quite happy to return to our more modest conditions. Most of the educated returned travellers, in fact, are very anxious to see the national coat being cut according to the national cloth and do not want 'development' to result in too much technological complication or society to be split into rich and poor. They will happily settle for an 'intermediate technology' in which men are still masters of the machines and I think they are right. There is nothing I admire more about our students than their general competence. In their world an adult man ought to be able to grow his own food, build his own house, catch his own fish, rear, kill and cook his own pig – and all our students can do all these things and intend to keep these skills even if they acquire enough book-learning to become graduates. If they can keep all this from the old way of life and at the same time break out of the conditions – ill-health, ignorance and sheer boredom – which have so often made that life nasty, brutish and short, they will be fortunate indeed and I shall not greatly repine at my lack of success in imparting to them the finer points of my native tongue.

VIII

FRIENDS AND NEIGHBOURS

At Kohimarama we seem to have a lot more friends and neighbours than we had at Siota. The nearest and dearest are the Brothers at Tabalia, five hundred yards down the road, where the Melanesian Brotherhood has its headquarters. The Melanesian Brotherhood must be one of the strangest religious communities in Christendom. It was founded in the 1920s by Ini Kopuria, an ex-policeman, for the purpose of evangelising the Solomon Islands. The idea was – and is – that young men should join the Brotherhood for a few years, going wherever they are sent and living in poverty, celibacy and obedience, and then return to ordinary life, probably marrying and settling down in their own villages. Brother Ini had some family land at Tabalia and he gave it to be the home and headquarters of the Brothers. For most of the time the Brothers are well away from Tabalia, living in households of three or four in the remaining heathen areas in the Solomons, some farther afield in the wild highlands of New Guinea, or in the New Hebrides and some as far away as Fiji, where they have established a household among the rural Indians in the sugar-growing area. These distant ventures seem to be due to the fact that they are running out of heathens to convert in the Solomons. But Tabalia is their home. 'Head Brother' lives there when he is not travelling (Brother Alan, the present Head Brother is a very fine and capable young man indeed, a New Hebridean), together with various other senior Brothers, notably Brother

71

Married to Melanesia

Wencelas, who is a rather fussed little man whose visits to us are associated with some unforeseen and often insoluble problem and who is inevitably known in our household as Good King Wenceslas. The novices spend two years at Tabalia before they are admitted to the Brotherhood and sent out. Some of them come from as far away as New Guinea or Fiji.

The Brotherhood is an entirely Melanesian institution with no European involvement, the only outsider being the chaplain, Brother Philip SSF, a Papuan Franciscan. They wear a uniform – they call it this rather than a habit – based on the costume of the native police in the twenties, black shirt, black 'calico' (the 'skirt' which ties round the waist) and a black and white cummerbund; thus attired, they are to be seen striding along the roads and paths, stick in hand, haversack on back, highly mobile and able to live off the land. Indeed, they do not reckon to buy food at all. They grow what they need, keep a few pigs and goats and sometimes go fishing. They also go hunting with a pack of half-starved dogs which range the neighbourhood by night, sniffing at our poultry through the chicken wire; these are generally somewhat unpopular neighbours.

Like most religious communities, the Brothers pray a good deal and they summon themselves to chapel by beating on a large old empty gas cylinder which gives out a booming noise audible for miles around; it is known in our household as the abbey bell. Their ideas of time are very approximate. Certain hours of the day they mark by beating their bell the appropriate number of times, for example three, but there is a margin of error of at least half an hour either way. This does not worry those of us who have our own clocks, but I must admit to a certain irritation when they mistake half past four for half past five in the early morning and the entire neighbourhood is aroused by the booming of their great bell. They themselves, however, like most Melanesians, probably do not care whether they get their night's sleep or not. David casually remarked to me one morning that he felt sleepy because he had been up all

Friends and Neighbours

night playing cards with 'some Brothers', which struck me as oddly unmonastic but did not greatly surprise me because I am, by now, used to the Brothers' idiosyncrasies.

Nearly all the Brothers are young, in their teens or twenties. Few of them have had much schooling. They are immensely tough; their way of life demands it. In some ways, I think they must be rather like the young men of the desert monasteries of the fourth century who were capable of providing a formidable bodyguard for any bishop their gang chose to support in the dangerous theological and political controversies of the time. Our Brothers have not been called upon to perform such offices – they release their aggression in Sunday morning football – but I would not care to be on the wrong side of them if fighting broke out.

Our other immediate neighbours are all villagers and it so happens that we live in the middle of a set of Catholic villages which partly accounts for the fact that we are not mother, father and Aunt Jane to the neighbourhood in anything like the same degree as we were in the Anglican purlieus of Gela, though they do tend to depend on us for transport in medical emergencies. We meet our village neighbours more in their capacity of market gardeners. Sometimes they do take their produce to Honiara to the market, but sometimes they cannot get transport or just want twenty cents to buy tobacco so they come to see if the Kohimarama staff will buy from them. Luke, Antonio and Menda are our real regulars. Luke has legs swollen with elephantiasis; he lives on the other side of our football field and he is always shuffling across with a pineapple or a few tomatoes and I nearly always buy his things whether I want them or not. Antonio is a rather superior person who handles larger sums of money and sometimes borrows a few dollars from Eric, always repaying them. It was he who built our rustic 'leaf' veranda. I never know what precisely he lives on, but he seems involved in litigation and land transfers. Menda is more down at heel. He is a rather pathetic widower with a row of little boys – seven or eight of them – in graduated sizes like organ pipes. These

Married to Melanesia

children sometimes appear at the door with produce in their hands, often a pawpaw clutched by the three-year-old. The ten-year-old, who has a fearsome squint, takes charge of the money. Their mother, who had a heart condition, died of the last baby, having been warned at the time of the previous one's birth that there should be no more. When we were told about this, we supported the doctor's advice that she should be sterilised, but they hesitated and felt they ought to get religious sanction from their own priest, who was, unfortunately, on leave at the time; nothing was done and the unfortunate woman died the following year. The widower takes it all stoically and indeed seems to make quite a good job of caring for the children.

Vatupilei, the next village farther in from the road, is the only Anglican village in the district and our relations with its people are rather closer, though they do, in fact, attend the Brothers' church at Tabalia where the services are more to their taste than ours and the sermons are always in pidgin. Here lives 'lime-boy', a young man who brings us juicy limes for a few cents a dozen. He suffers appallingly from a disfiguring skin-disease known locally as *bakua* and I often wish that he would consume some of his own limes, having a vague association in my mind of scurvy with his kind of trouble, though I now discover that it is in fact a fungal infection and Nonie Connor's assertion that soap and water was the best cure might not have been so far wrong. 'Lime-boy', whose name turned out to be Ngai, struck up a friendship with Dudley who came over from Gela with the Connors as David did with us, and Dudley fell in love with Ngai's sister and she with him. They were determined to marry but the girl's parents and the elders generally forbade it. The only thing against Dudley was that he was a Gela man; in all other respects one would have thought that he would have been a most eligible son-in-law, young, healthy, good-looking and of proven industrious habits. George Connor went to see the elders to plead Dudley's cause, but he had no luck at all. Then the couple eloped. David, who

Friends and Neighbours

had been in the secret, told me all about it with a lot of circumstantial detail. They had, it seemed, set out for Honiara on Friday night at 10.35 precisely; he was very particular about the time. The girl was not missed till next morning when the elders came storming up to Kohimarama demanding from David where Dudley was. David was fairly sure the couple were on a ship for Gela by this time, but he stalled and a long scene followed with dramatic conversation. The finest line I remember from David's vivid account was, 'Where we find Dudley, there we bury Dudley.' Luckily, it did not come to that. Dudley took his girl to Boromole and left her with his people, returning very honourably to face the family, bearing the bride-price with him, all fair and square. After a lot more negotiation and the summoning of more and more relatives from farther along Guadalcanal, the family acquiesced in the *fait accompli* but young Lochinvar had to find yet *more* bride-price as a fine for his high-handed action. It was on this occasion that for some reason – perhaps because the Connors had not enough money in the house and it was at the weekend – that we were appealed to for a loan of twenty dollars to close the deal. We were approached through David who told Dudley that it would be necessary to ask 'father' because 'Mrs Jones only has small money for tomatoes' (not big money for brides). This choice *obiter dictum* has gone down in our family as a description of loose change, of which Eric does, indeed, regularly clear his pockets and which I scoop up for chaffering with 'ravens' at the door. David presumably thinks I am only trusted with money in any quantity when I go to Honiara on my own.

The Catholic villages around us all look to Visale as their centre. This is a big mission station on the main road four or five miles beyond our turning. It is presided over by Father Kennedy (a New Zealander but so Irish that it is not true), who is very good at all the practical missionary things such as building, so that they have an enormous fine church, several houses and a clinic all built under his supervision in concrete bricks; he is now helping the villagers to build themselves an

75

Married to Melanesia

equally durable community centre of fantastic design. He is a friendly and hospitable man and glad that since the Second Vatican Council he is officially supposed to be on good terms with us separated brethren, but still a bit bewildered to find that we are no longer just heretics, at least not in quite the same sense that we were when he left his seminary. I doubt if he has had much time, among all his multifarious chores, in more recent years to do much reading and catch up with the present climate of thought in these matters.

Visale also houses a large community of nuns, who supervise a primary boarding school, run a clinic with a labour ward for simple maternity work, and also look after the aged members of their own community, some of whom are quite senile and all of whom are disabled in some way and constitute a very heavy responsibility for the younger ones. I once made the mistake of replying in French to one of these old, old ladies who was quite blind and came shuffling along a veranda on which I was sitting waiting for a patient and nearly fell over me. 'Qui êtes-vous?' she demanded, and my incautious reply landed us in a dreadful linguistic and ecumenical tangle. We like the Superior, Sister Marie Fernand, who left her native Britanny some forty-odd years ago, and recently returned from one of her very infrequent leaves having been much bamboozled by taxi-drivers in Rome and having disliked what she saw in France, disapproving, *inter alia* of the Breton independence movement. She is, improbably, an expert with a gun. One of the other Sisters, an American, was presented by her brother in the States with a revolver for self-defence. (Luckily, we do not need such things here, in fact.) It arrived by post and gave a good deal of trouble in the customs, but in the end it was duly licensed and brought out to Visale, where Sister Marie Fernand appears to have said, like Lady Macbeth, 'Give me the dagger!' I gather that she personally shoots, from time to time, one of their cows for them to eat. These cows are a prosperous and prolific herd; they seem to be quite successfully managed as a general thing by schoolgirls.

Friends and Neighbours

Also at Visale is the novitiate of the Daughters of Mary Immaculate (DMIs for short), an entirely Melanesian religious community but with an Australian novice-mistress who is another of our friends. We tend to refer to the DMIs as 'the Daughters' and are often struck by the very Melanesian quality of their life which contrasts oddly with their fairly conventional, if simplified, religious habit of dark blue dress, white veil and pectoral cross. They are quite often to be seen, fully dressed, veil and all, wading out on the reef catching fish, up to their waists in the sea. They have acquired other dashing skills of a more European kind; quite a number of them can and do drive trucks and tractors. They do a good deal of teaching and general parish work, housekeeping in the Catholic guest-house in Honiara and all kinds of practical things. I was talking to some of them one evening at a party in Honiara in honour of one of the (European) Anglican Sisters who had just been solemnly professed, and was asking them how they had come to join the Daughters. They said it had been very hard, especially for the Malaitans, and usually against family resistance, for the families lost their immediate labour and the prospect of a bride-price and grandchildren. But they were obviously girls of great character and they had persisted and won. They were a good deal more cheerful and merry than many of the young married women one sees about and I could not help thinking that in their place I would myself prefer being a nun to being the slave of the average Malaitan husband. Women's Lib in these parts can take surprising forms.

Relations between us and Visale were not always so warm and indeed the Catholic and Anglican villages around us seem to have been in a state of feud until quite recent years. (There was, actually, an unhappy history in the twenties and thirties which accounts for this.) During our first year at Kohimarama, we were knocked up at four o'clock one morning by the Anglican villagers from Vatupilei demanding that we should take a woman who was in labour to 'Number Nine', the Central Hospital in Honiara. Our little truck, then the only vehicle on

Married to Melanesia

the station, happened to have no unpunctured spare tyre and, as the road is always completely deserted at night and Eric had no wish to set off for Honiara, have a puncture and find himself delivering the woman by the roadside or in the middle of a river, he offered to take her down to Visale where the Sisters have their little labour ward. The men went away and returned at seven o'clock saying that the baby had been born but the placenta was retained. Would Mrs Connor come and cope? Nonie was herself at the time in bed in the course of a difficult pregnancy and quite incapable of a two-mile walk in the bush, even if she had had the equipment for the job, which she had not. She sent the men back to the village with a stretcher and told them to bring the woman back with them and somebody would drive her down to Visale where the Sisters were equipped to deal with a retained placenta. Nothing more was heard for three days, at the end of which the Brothers, asked to enquire, brought back the welcome news that all was well, nature had taken its course, and the woman had not died. The people, they said, had absolutely refused to go to Visale because Vatupilei was an Anglican village and the Sisters were Catholics.

This made us rather impotently angry, but after two or three more years of obvious friendliness between the two mission staffs, the atmosphere has changed. On the first Monday of the month when a doctor visits Visale, we take the college truck down for his clinic, fairly bulging with 'olgeta woman' and 'olgeta piccaniny' – students' wives and children, village wives and children, gathering them up *en route*, for their immunisations against polio, smallpox, measles, etc., and their ante-natal and post-natal examinations. Most normal births now take place at Visale. We pack the woman in labour, husband and often a toddler into the car, stow away various bags of *kumara* (sweet potato), a Primus stove and cooking pots, and a lamp and kerosene in the boot and off we go. Return journey three days later. No trouble. And the Catholic villagers come to our feasts and we go to theirs.

Friends and Neighbours

The latest development has been to start a joint primary school – hitherto unheard of – at Tanakuku just across our football field, which flourishes exceedingly and has solved for us an acute problem about the education of our students' younger school-age children. Teachers have been provided by both Churches and the young men seem to share their houses amicably enough. The Daughters and our students share the religious education, not on the basis of Anglicans to the left, Catholics to the right, but all together. And our students run Cubs and Brownies for the children. David's little nephew, John Selwyn, has come over from Gela to live with him for the sake of the school and I hear a good many multiplication tables and other feats of memory being practised around the house and garden of an afternoon. He is the leading singer, having an unusually sweet voice, in the Cub pack which enters – and wins – an annual singing competition in Honiara with John Selwyn wielding the baton. Great are the efforts David and I put into the neckerchief and the shirt and the shorts for this occasion.

The school is run by a committee of parents (in practice, fathers) who look after the buildings and grow some of the food for the children. Every year there is an 'education week' when all hands are on deck all week, building a new classroom or a new teacher's house or starting a new garden and everybody takes part – men, women and children. The school opened with one class at the end of one such annual effort. On Monday we saw people going by with posts and 'leaf' and work was obviously in full swing all week; but we were astounded to be summoned on the Saturday afternoon to the opening of the school and told that classes would start on the following Monday. Father Kennedy (in lace cotta and with incense) and Eric (caught unawares in shirt and shorts) blessed it all between them and we then sat down to a feast with speeches from the local notables. The secretary to the 'board of governors' is a local young man – a Catholic – by the name of Abadon (pronounced Ambadon). His brother is called

Married to Melanesia

Ubaldo, which I imagine is the name of some obscure Italian saint imported by the early Catholic missionaries. Abadon can surely only be Abaddon, the Angel of the Pit in Revelation. It does seem odd to give anybody a patron demon as opposed to a patron saint, but we have noticed before in the Pacific and among Protestants that a name only needs to be biblical to be sanctified; it does not matter whether the character concerned was a goodie or a baddie. A Goliath applied – unsuccessfully – for entrance to our college one year. Abadon has been to secondary school and speaks good English, but he seems to be a gentleman of leisure, who lives in the village, writes letters for people, negotiates with Europeans and government officials and generally behaves like a young squire. We often wonder why he does not do a job, but I daresay he is as usefully employed oiling the local works as he would be pushing a pen in Honiara. What he lives on I have no idea, though I do know that we sometimes have to invent jobs for his brother Ubaldo to do in order to pay him a month's wage to enable him to find his tax.

Our most continuous body of friends and neighbours is, I suppose, 'The Carpenters', although they do not technically live near us on a permanent basis. We have had building in progress ever since we arrived at Kohimarama. No contractor from Honiara will come out on our roads and over our rivers and so everything has had to be built by the diocesan works department which has its headquarters at Taroaniara on Gela. 'Olgeta carpenter' *are* basically carpenters, though they turn their hands to masonry and plumbing and have even erected the new octagonal chapel, learning as they went, on a massive steel frame supplied by the makers like a Meccano set to be assembled. But they are best at working in wood, which is one reason why our concrete box of a house is less successful than later efforts built on a timber frame with a raised wood floor. For much of the time we have had two gangs with a foreman each. They work very well with very little supervision, though they have trouble – and only sometimes on account of lack of

Friends and Neighbours

foresight – in assembling their building materials. Most of them are related to some of the students or their wives; many have been at the diocese's primary boarding schools with students. So they are very much part of the family. They play football against the students and Brothers on a Sunday morning and sometimes reinforce the students' team with their star players in the Honiara league matches on Saturday afternoons.

They are nearly all young bachelors and they live (except for the older foreman, Alan, who with his wife and children occupies one of the students' married quarters) in what must be a dreadful barracks they have run up for themselves in corrugated iron, down by the river where they sometimes get flooded out. We lay on a monthly shopping trip in the truck for them after pay-day and they return with sacks of rice, tins of fish and such strangely popular things as tins of cocoa and Milo, singing cheerfully. Singing and listening to the radio are seemingly their principal pleasures and their musical tastes are remarkably catholic. On a single morning I have heard drifting over from the building site Viennese waltzes (picked up from a record programme on the radio), 'Oh, no John!', 'Early one morning', 'The holly and the ivy', a set of *Kyries*, 'The sweet nightingale', and any amount of current pop from such sources as 'Olgeta Temptations' or 'Olgeta Beatles' as the Solomon Islands Broadcasting Service describes them.

The SIBS, for an outfit run on a shoestring and not too efficiently at that, must be about the most popular radio service in the world. It has, of course, no competition. There are no newspapers or magazines and precious few books, but few villages can be without at least one transistor radio. Broadcasting also has many practical uses. Shipping is warned of high seas and storms and in cyclone weather everybody's ears are glued to the radio, listening for the latest details of the path of the hurricane and calculating whether it will hit one in force and at what time. Government departments put out daily announcements as do the churches, alerting teachers, medical assistants or villagers generally to the fact that a ship will be

81

Married to Melanesia

calling at such and such a place at such and such a time for such and such a purpose. Will the whole community be ready to meet a committee of the Governing Council to discuss the proposed new constitution? Will teacher X be ready to go to Honiara? Will the district nurse assemble everybody with eye trouble to be seen by a visiting doctor? These 'Service Messages' are followed by the 'Paid Announcements', which include such items as 'X has been accepted as a student at Kohimarama. Will he please make his own way to Y by January Z and wait there for a ship to pick him up?' or even, 'David Mala is coming home for the wedding. Will Silas of Belaga please bring a canoe to Taroaniara to meet him?' It is a more reliable and infinitely more rapid method of communication than letters and it contributes to the general sense in the country that, scattered as we are, we all know each other's business. And it is all done in English and then in pidgin. As is the news.

The BBC overseas news is relayed once a day but bad reception often makes it almost unintelligible. The Australian news usually comes over more clearly and this is what we listen to. But the local news is really obligatory if one wants to know what is going on and we try never to miss a day. Its arrangement defies every principle of order to which one has been trained, items about important new economic developments or constitutional change lying cheek-by-jowl with sheer chat about a man being chased up a tree by a wild pig, or a ghost appearing in a rest house, or a three-headed pineapple being grown. Feasts and weddings are reported in blow-by-blow detail and we have often been entertained by accounts of weddings which record the exact number of parcels of pudding consumed and the number of pigs slaughtered and fish caught, then go on to give an account of the football match that followed but omit at any stage to mention who married whom. Perhaps that is the least important feature. There are schools broadcasts and a Sunday play, to which Eric and I ritually listen, whatever it is. Sometimes it is serialised on two successive Sundays, but with a bit of luck the man who is managing the

Friends and Neighbours

tape goes out for a smoke and leaves it running so that we get the *dénouement* at the first go. Our absolute favourites are actually shorter, being a Sherlock Holmes series, long-super-annuated from the BBC, which has given us our domestic slogan, 'Let us return to our humble abode'.

But to return to 'olgeta carpenter'. Their taste, like David's and nearly everybody else's, is emphatically for pop and this is what the SIBS mostly provides. They all write in for their 'requests' as does, I should guess, practically every literate person in the country – quite half of the local letters dropped into our mailbag for posting seem to be addressed to the SIBS – and I have often found myself in demand to type out a list of pop song titles, wildly guessing what they must be, from bits of paper on which people have phonetically written down what they think they have heard the disc jockey say. It has been an education for me.

IX

RELIGION

Years of experience as an expatriate Christian had, I thought, cured me of any preconceptions about the forms the Christian religion might take long before I embarked on my belated career as a missionary wife. In my time I have worshipped in a White Fathers' church in Northern Ghana – this was some twenty years ago – with a congregation clad for the most part in holy medals and loin cloths or even leaves, and have been touched, as well as amused, by the pious attitudes of the nearly naked old ladies receiving holy communion with the same devout composure customary in old ladies throughout Christendom. It did cross my mind to imagine the surprise of their co-religionists in Italy or Spain who have, from time to time, been outraged by my own bare arms in their church buildings. As a passing motorist I have been held up in a Ghana town by a gay Easter procession of Methodists, freely flinging talcum powder around and dowsing me with it by way of friendly compliment to a stranger. What crossed my mind on that occasion was that *their* English co-religionists might not have approved of the principle of making a joyful smell before the Lord, or they would have passed on a tradition of incense, so much more agreeable and less clinging than cheap talc.

As for my fellow-Anglicans, they come in so many varieties that I have long since stopped believing what they used to say in Sunday school, namely that it will be just like home in church on whatever exotic shore you find yourself. True, the services usually have a general resemblance to the Book of Common Prayer – though all this is noticeably falling apart

Religion

these days and, in my opinion, hardly a moment too soon. In addition, most Anglican cathedrals up and down the world can mount a Sunday morning occasion suitable for a Royal Visit, with Prince Philip reading the lessons, and very nice too. But those who have not strayed further than this from the Anglican tourist routes have seen little – though even they may have seen the vast matrons of Accra, bulging cheerfully out of their richest brocades and velvets, surmounted by hats, sweating under a blazing sun and singing Hymns Ancient and Modern with a gusto rare under our northern skies. Not always with accuracy. I remember standing in the fierce pressure of crowded Palm Sunday congregation in Accra Cathedral next to a large lady who sang, all unaware,

'Ride on, ride on in magistrate,
Hark all the tribes Hosanna cry,'

and wondering if her mental picture of the original scene was set under the British colonial raj.

But the real nitty-gritty – in Africa or Melanesia – is remote from the airports and the jets, in the village churches, where strange cultural transmutations occur. Before I came to the Solomons, an English friend, a monk and historian, begged me to ascertain if it was indeed true that altar frontals are to be seen here in impeccable Victorian taste and colours but bearing the embroidered legend TABU TABU TABU. I found this thought almost as comic as he did at the time, but it is true, and it no longer strikes me as particularly odd because I too have assimilated the Pacific concept of 'tabu' as meaning anything from 'Holy' to 'No Entry' or 'Trespassers Will Be Prosecuted' or even (when scratched on a palm tree) 'Do not pick the coconuts; they are not yours.'

Solomon Islanders are very religious. In their heathen days they had many 'customs' which they performed in connection with their daily activities – fishing, hunting or starting a new garden – as well as in the crises of human life, birth, marriage and death. The new religion, Christianity, is expected to be at

Married to Melanesia

least as efficacious as the old and its rites assume a similarly central place in everyday life. From a Christian point of view, this attitude to religion has disadvantages as well as the more obvious merits. Until very recently, most people have been illiterate, so there has hardly been a Bible-reading or a very reflective Church. Moreover the vast multiplicity of languages has too often resulted in a half-understood religion largely conducted in an unfamiliar tongue and done for you by somebody else – the priest or the catechist or even some half-educated village reader just capable of stumbling through the words of morning or evening prayer. But people certainly go to church – at any rate in the villages – many of them morning and evening to have the community's religion performed. In the towns, where this is impracticable on account of people's working day, there is apt to be much head-shaking, not because people do not go to church on Sunday, but because they do not go every day. Europeans are inexplicable. Many of them do not even go to church on Sunday, and there has been much criticism of the young overseas volunteers who have helped to staff the schools because they have often found daily church-going too much for them; they are, in most cases, going to church oftener than they ever did in their young lives, but it still seems pitifully inadequate to their Solomon Islands colleagues and pupils.

We live in a theological centre, where by European standards you might expect to find rather a concentration of religion. In fact, there is little more – in terms of the community's time – than in a village, though, having the generator to give us light, we are able to devote the period from quarter to six to half past six in the morning to worship in church and to postpone our evening prayer to the dusk hour of quarter to six in the evening. And, being theological students, we are professionally concerned with worship, aware of new thinking on the subject and very much more likely to experiment and change things than the very traditional village congregations.

When we arrived at Siota, this was hardly true. We were

86

Religion

warned that Melanesia was ultra-conservative and the slightest change was liable to give grave offence. A great many pious customs had grown up and Eric was anxious to do a little necessary pruning, but he moved slowly, waiting till he felt he knew the students and they him. A source of special irritation to the Joneses was the Angelus – not that we had any particular objection to it in itself; indeed, the mid-day and evening bell momentarily raising people's hearts to God in the midst of the work of life has an obvious attraction and value. But with us the mid-day Angelus hopelessly disrupted the last lecture of the morning, the whole class leaping piously to its feet as the words died on the lecturer's lips and the train of thought petered out irrecoverably. The evening Angelus was worse as it caught us on our way back to the house after evensong in the chapel. Everybody froze in their tracks and the warden's wife – still less the warden – could not without scandal keep moving homewards, though one felt disposed to cry out, 'I've prayed enough! I've just finished!' One notable occasion stands out in my memory. I had been ill in hospital in Honiara and had come back to Gela on a diocesan ship returning to Taroaniara, its home port. Taking pity on my still convalescent state, Brian Ayers, in charge at Taroaniara, had very kindly sent the ship on, another hour's sailing, to Siota in order to get me home the same day. As we reached the end of the Boli Passage and Siota came into view, I saw the students coming out of chapel at the end of evensong. I was just thinking, 'Oh, good. There'll be people around to catch a rope and tie us up' (for there was a vicious current just by our wharf which was apt to swing ships round and smash the timbers of the jetty if nobody was ashore to give a hand), when the Angelus bell rang. The students, who had been running down to the wharf, piously froze; the warden's wife, helpless on deck, uttered blasphemies; and the *Baddeley* went crashing into the jetty.

Another occasion at Siota when religion collided with com-mon sense was one evening when we were all in chapel at even-song and the *Baddeley* was heard, and then seen, approaching

Married to Melanesia

the wharf. This time, Eric ran out of church, caught a rope and helped to tie the ship up. She had brought our quarterly stores; sacks of sugar, flour and rice, cartons of tinned meat and fish, drums of kerosene and diesel oil for the lights and the generator. We were all pleased and rather relieved to see her as stocks had run very low. The ship's crew, anxious to get back to their port, Taroaniara, as soon after nightfall as possible, started to unload the cargo themselves as nobody else appeared to do it, and the wharf was soon full of sacks. But the students went on praying. Then it began to rain. The office of evensong was actually over, but the student officiant went on praying for this and that. Finally, Eric could bear it no more. He returned angrily to the chapel and interrupted the excessive and untimely devotion to point out that unless somebody quickly went down and got the flour and sugar under cover we should have no proper daily bread for the next three months, let us pray for it as earnestly as we might, and serve us all right. The point was taken, the food was rescued and the crew were able to sail off home.

Our move to Kohimarama was the occasion of many breaks with past tradition, not least in the community's religious habits. I was amused at Eric's opportunism. Custom, as many anthropologists have observed, is King in the Pacific, and Eric succeeded in several directions, as soon as we arrived at Kohimarama, in mesmerising the community into accepting that this or that 'is our custom here!' The first evening that we were all assembled at Kohimarama, we were standing about, staff and students, chatting in the sunset after evensong when the timekeeper for the week was seen approaching the bell to ring the Angelus. His hand was actually raised when the warden rushed up, saying blandly, 'Oh, Barnabas, it is not our custom here to ring the Angelus.' Barnabas (it happened to be the very man who had prayed so intemperately at Siota while the flour got wet) was puzzled but the word 'custom' worked like a charm and we have had no Angelus since.

Another more significant swinging of custom concerned the

Religion

seating in chapel. At Siota we had a roomy church and the students occupied more than their fair share of it, sitting choir-wise, facing each other and sideways on to the altar. At the back of the church there were also rows of seats, facing the altar, for non-students, men on the right, women on the left. We wives were packed together with the children in the hottest and sunniest corner of the church and swarmed over by babies and toddlers (two to each wife on an average). Village habit brought the women twice daily to church, though most of them can hardly have understood a word that passed even if the babies had not made it impossible for them to pay any attention. The semi-monastic arrangement of the seating was, admittedly, a special feature of the Siota tradition, but the separation of men and women is normal in all but a few town churches and follows Melanesian custom, by which all public social intercourse tends to be a one-sex affair. This strikes us as sub-Christian and it is, in any case, clearly going to change quite rapidly with new ideas about social and family life coming in as some of the new generation of girls are educated. For these reasons, we felt rather strongly that the church ought not to be encouraging its future leaders to follow this custom by separating them from their families in chapel during their training. Besides, two parents have some hope of controlling two under-fours; one parent has none. So as soon as we arrived at Kohimarama where the church was not arranged like a cathedral or a monastic choir, Eric blandly announced yet again, 'It is our custom here that families sit together.' They have meekly done this ever since, and some of the women have, indeed, recognised that twice-daily attendance at church is not necessary for salvation either for them or their babies and that nobody thinks the worse of them if they do not show up every time. Furthermore, we have been pleased to see that some of the fathers occasionally stay at home with the children to give their wives an opportunity for a little unencumbered worship, a thing that would have been unthinkable in the semi-monastic ambience of the Siota piety.

Married to Melanesia

We think that the families like sitting together. Certainly Melanesian men, as well as women, manifest every sign of enjoying the company of young children. Even the single men go out of their way to play with other people's babies, carrying them around and generally making much of them. Families are large and long. At the moment, the Solomon Islands do not need to fear an immediate population explosion and indeed an increase in population would probably be beneficial. But we feel some concern about the mothers, who certainly have too many babies at too frequent intervals for their own good and, tragically, sometimes die of the eighth or ninth. This applies to educated and uneducated people alike and we have often marvelled at the patience – indeed positive pleasure – with which people like our Melanesian colleagues will live for twenty years at a stretch with young children continuously under their feet. Perhaps we are unduly sour, and certainly we are very unfashionable, but when it comes to public worship we have been gradually coming round to the view of the Scottish kirk which, we are told, used to employ beadles to silence the 'greeting of bairns' and Eric has been known, after a sore trial, to declare darkly that he will adopt King Herod as his patron saint, as he sings a snatch of his favourite Christmas carol which goes, 'And slew the little childer, and *slew* the little childer.'

The students' children and those of the neighbourhood actually serve as very useful practice material for the religious education course. Every Sunday morning there is a Sunday school conducted by the students for these small things aged from three to seven or so, and we listen to the proceedings from our house. (We cannot help it; the chapel at Kohimarama is within easy earshot of our living room.) Teaching has to be in pidgin, being the nearest approach to a *lingua franca*, but most of the songs are in English. A favourite song has always been 'Our Sunday school is over, and we are going home. Goodbye! Goodbye!' and we have often wondered if the children had any conception of the meaning since at one time

Religion

it was habitually sung, apparently by spontaneous impulse, as they assembled. Before we had a religious education expert on the staff, the lessons themselves were often deplorable. There was a series which went on for weeks that we called 'The Naming of Parts'. It consisted of trailing the children round the church building and talking about the lectern, font, altar, and so on. Within reason, this might have had some limited validity, but it was much overdone and we could hardly believe our ears the week the student in charge gravely led the three-year-olds through the mysteries of the Service Register in the vestry, solemnly instructing them to make sure to sign in the book after every service. Since then there has been a great reformation and the children now run wild according to the best modern education theory and sing action songs, which we enjoy. Sunday school always has been very popular (the children who attend are also welcome at the community breakfast of bread, jam and sweet tea, which foods are an exotic treat for some of them). It takes strange forms nowadays, as when I found a mob of twenty or thirty four-year-olds round my front door in the middle of the proceedings, having been sent, they said, to 'look at pussycat'. They had come to the right house; we usually have a plethora.

We are told by our students that most village people are excessively traditionalist about religion. They are not the only ones in Christendom of whom this would be true, but it does seem that in Melanesia the Church is heir to an attitude to 'custom' which reinforces the normal conservatism of Christians. In the old heathen days, religious observance was the specialist activity of the 'custom' priest with his 'custom' house. Certain words had to be said and certain actions performed and it was important to get them exactly right. The liturgy and ritual of the Church tends to be thought of in a similar way, so that when the diocese of Melanesia, in common with most of contemporary Christendom, embarked on a programme of modest liturgical change a few years ago, many village congregations, especially on the very traditionalist island of Malaita

Married to Melanesia

were very disturbed; they felt that the new words and gestures might not 'work'. God would not respond.

Similarly, there are some very fixed ideas about proper clothing. The early missionaries must have imported rolls of white calico, and the first Solomon Islanders to wear clothes at all simply replaced the grass skirt or strip of bark cloth with a length of calico fastened round the waist. ('Calico' is still the ordinary word in pidgin for any kind of clothes.) In these more sophisticated days, men are likely to wear, for best, a pair of shorts and a shirt, but the idea of white clothing – presumably based on the original white calico – as the proper dress for Sunday church-going dies very hard. I was puzzled by David's asking me once, in the early days of our association, if I would mend his holy communion trousers on my sewing machine. These turned out to be his white shorts. The villagers who came across the Passage from Boromole to worship in our church at Siota on Sunday mornings used to paddle across in their canoes wearing their scruffiest clothes and change into their holy communion trousers in the shelter of an outhouse under our bedroom window. The women would put on two extra skirts on top of the three they were already wearing.

One of the two Melanesian bishops, Dudley Tuti, told us about finding a notice in a village church in his area written in a language he understood, and 'signed', though not by him, ✠ DUDLEY, to the effect that anybody presenting himself to receive holy communion not wearing white trousers would be turned away. Needless to say, he tore the notice down and administered a rebuke, but the incident is indicative of the feeling in many communities about the traditional 'customs'.

Despite all this, we have found our theological students surprisingly open, ready to think about their religion and quite prepared to consider change. They are much more responsible in their attitude to the 'people back home' than their Western counterparts, prepared to reason and experiment themselves but well aware of the difficulty of changing anything in the village and not wanting to rush in like a bull in a china shop.

Religion

They say that they think that Christian worship in the past has been too European and they are anxious to try out Melanesian forms while they are still in this protected environment where an experiment that fails is not a disaster. A successful occasion when something was tried out was the consecration of our new chapel – our first permanent church building – when the Bishop asked that the students and the Melanesian staff should themselves devise a form of service. They entered into this with enthusiasm and adapted various traditional customs, using some of the symbolism which their ancestors associated with making a house 'tabu' or holy. For example, the Bishop's first act before he or anybody else entered the building was to plant a sprig of a particular aromatic shrub outside, being a symbolic protection of the place from bad spirits. During the service clouds of incense arose, nor from a brass thurible swung by a young man in a cotta but from a firepot in the middle of the church on to which handfuls of incense, scraped from the bark of local trees, were tossed from time to time. The students and the Melanesian staff chose to dress for the occasion in traditional costume – a loincloth made of bark with faces and bodies painted with lime in careful patterns, this being a traditional sign of ceremony. It was a deeply moving occasion and clearly meaningful for those who had devised it and took part in it. I wondered how it would be received by the simple-minded and old-fashioned villagers who were also present, but the students told us afterwards that many of these had expressed satisfaction and appreciation and had seemed to find meaning in it. This was an indication, to my mind, that the people are not so mindlessly conservative as has sometimes been suggested. It has, however, to be said on the other side that there was some public indignation expressed in Honiara towards the Church's regrettable reversion to 'heathen custom'. These people had not themselves been present but had heard the occasion described on the radio. And this suggests the existence of a problem here which is quite as old as that of St Augustine of Canterbury among the Anglo-Saxons converting the ancient

Married to Melanesia

places of heathen worship to Christian uses on the gentle advice of Pope Gregory the Great; or St Boniface in Germany doing the opposite thing and hacking down the sacred oaks; it is a problem that any people must, in the end, solve for itself.

Successive generations of students have expressed concern about another difficulty, the fact that bread and wine, the universal matter of the universal Christian sacrament, are totally unfamiliar forms of food and drink in Solomon Island villages. The itinerant district priest has to carry them round with him; they could not possibly be provided, as our English prayer book has directed since the sixteenth century, by the people and they cannot bear the symbolism of normal food and drink. A few radical souls will usually propose at this point that the matter of the sacrament should be changed in the islands to boiled kumara which is the people's 'daily bread' and coconut juice or even water, the normal drink. (Solomon Islanders are the first people I have known without an indigenous alcoholic drink.) One year, this was felt so strongly that the Bishop's permission was sought and given for an experiment along these lines within the college community. But it turned out to be an experiment which nobody, not even its keenest promoters, supported for more than a few weeks. What the Melanesian Church should do about this I have no idea, but I am certain that they will not find their own way in this difficult field of adaptation until they are really on their own and feel themselves fully autonomous. Our students' readiness to think the unthinkable and try things out has encouraged us to hope that they are not for ever stuck with the rather old-fashioned and very European stereotypes which we found when we arrived at Siota. Surely God wants to see his people doing their own thing and not for ever imitating something alien to themselves.

X

BEASTS

Looking back over our five Melanesian years, I am struck by the important part that beasts of various kinds have played in our life: beasts that we have kept and which have given us a quite disproportionate pleasure and amusement, beasts we have regularly passed the time of day with, and the fauna generally of the countryside.

We have no lions or tigers or elephants or giraffes – not even apes and monkeys. The bush has wild pigs, which I have never seen but have eaten at feasts at the Brothers' who hunt them. The Brothers also hunt the harmless opossum, which seems rather a shame. These too find their way into feasts and it can be disconcerting to open one's banana-leaf parcel of baked meat only to disclose what looks uncommonly like a baby's hand.

Sharks infest the sea between Gela and Guadalcanal and they are man-eaters. They are said to have developed a taste for human flesh at the time of the great naval battle of the Second World War between the Japanese and the Americans, when Iron Bottom Sound, still full of rusting wrecks as the name implies, provided them with some grim feasting. People do not, on the whole, bathe in this sea but sometimes the sharks come a little way up the numerous Guadalcanal rivers and take a victim, usually a woman or a child unwarily doing the family wash.

Crocodiles are also known in our rivers. There was a radio news item recently about an acquaintance of ours, a teacher, who was out with some schoolgirls in a canoe which was

The crocodile pool at Tanaemba

Beasts

persistently pursued by a crocodile; with a spirit worthy of the nineteenth-century pioneer missionaries, she beat the creature off with her umbrella. We actually have a family of crocodiles within the clan at Kohimarama, or rather just down our river at Tanaemba. They inhabit a highly picturesque small lagoon at the mouth of the Tanaemba River. Our Sunday afternoon walk usually takes us along the shore to the mouth of this river which is partly blocked by a sandbar, and at this point we turn our backs on the sea and gaze across the crocodile pool towards the distant mountain, often at that hour cloud-capped. The whole prospect might have been laid out by Capability Brown – except that the vegetation is mostly coconut palms. These, however, are leaning in attitudes of self-conscious elegance, reflected in the still waters of the pool, especially two noble specimens, apparently strategically positioned on an island at the top end of the pool – itself beautifully laid out and gracefully wooded, all by Nature – with the mountain beyond, a triumph of perspective. Occasionally, someone will paddle a canoe slowly across the lagoon and one fancies that the scene has shifted from our eighteenth-century gentleman's park to a print of the noble savage illustrating some book in his library. But to the locals, it is just the crocodile pool, home of a dynasty of crocodiles whose forebears had close totemic relations with the people's ancestors. They tell us that the crocodiles would never dream of hurting us locals and we, for our part, do not seek their skins for handbags. But if, as often happens, one of the young ones leaves the sanctuary of the ancestral pool and makes up our river, he is usually caught and skinned. One of our colleagues kept one as a pet; this I could not fancy doing.

Snakes, a familiar feature of my West African life, are rare in the Solomons. Our worst domestic enemy, apart from rats, is the centipede. We never had one of these in the Siota house, which was well up off the ground, but we have had them in the little concrete bungalow at Kohimarama. Once caught sight of, they must be pursued and killed as their sting is among the

Married to Melanesia

most painful of animal injuries and would certainly be lethal to kittens – and possibly to the cat – who always want to hunt and play with a centipede. I once saw one out of the corner of my eye on the living room wall at half past five in the morning when I was making an early cup of tea. Jenny, our cat, also saw it and began to stalk it. It promptly disappeared, with me in hot pursuit, behind the furniture. Eric rushed out of the bathroom to help. A bewildered visitor from New Zealand came out of the spare room in his pyjamas to see what we were up to and within a few minutes we had the room upside down, the cat expelled through one door and the current kitten family through another and all three human beings thrashing about in mortal terror for our bare feet until the visitor finally got the beast with a shoe and hacked it into messy pieces all over the sofa cover and cushions, which were by now on the floor. These epic encounters with the more horrid of God's creatures – I have had similar feelings in fights with outsize cockroaches in Africa – always stir in me vague undergraduate memories of the struggle of Beowulf with Grendel; I have been surprised to find myself shouting inaccurate snatches of Anglo-Saxon verse, which is surprising as I never, in the far off days when I sat under Professor Tolkien, much cared for the stuff; it is not really my style. Perhaps it is the black liquid – blood? – which they exude. '*Wyrm hat gemealt*' or 'The hot worm melted', as Beowulf, I think, says. And was not the worm a type of devil?

Another menace, but one we do not feel called upon to deal with, is the flying foxes or fruit-bats. I have only once seen a flying-fox close enough to examine it and this was in the Healesville Sanctuary in Victoria in Australia. I was astonished by its head, which is indeed just like that of a fox. It was daytime and it was hanging asleep in its cage. But we have flying-foxes all round the house at Kohimarama, unseen but very noisy at night. They seem to lack the ordinary bat's built-in radar and they blunder into things – clothes lines, water pipes from the guttering into the tank, that sort of thing – making a

Beasts

constant twanging and clatter. They also seem to argue and fight a good deal among themselves. They come for our mangoes and our sour-sops and always get a bigger share of these fruits than we do, spoiling more than they eat. We once had a temporary houseboy, Moffat, who was much out with his bow and arrows. I was curious to know what he was after and rather surprised, though not displeased, when it turned out to be flying-foxes, which he averred were good eating.

Lizards – small geckoes – on the other hand are almost domestic pets. The Kohimarama house is the first of my tropical homes where they have especially proliferated in the kitchen. Here, I have whole families of them on my store shelves and they and I are often startled when I reach out for a tin and pick up a lizard with it. They have a strange, transparent look about them, prominent beady eyes and the most astonishing, scoop-shaped, bright red tongues. I have watched one for five minutes licking up some almost invisible food-splash off a window sill with its busy red tongue bent over backwards nearly double, scraping away.

Bird life is especially rich and various. We see many splendid birds on our walks, notably the red cardinal and the greenish-white parakeet, both of which seem to like coconut groves as a home. Not so many birds come round our house, though the hibiscus flowers in the garden are visited by minute little green honey-eaters which hang upside down with their beaks in the flowers, sucking out the sweetness. But most of the birds, especially the parrots which are numerous in the valley below, are shy and rarely seen but incessantly heard, even at night. They are great mimics. There is one known as the 'pussycat bird' which has repeatedly fooled us into thinking we had a kitten in trouble somewhere near the house. And when Sean Connor was teething and cried often and loudly, we developed a 'Sean bird' whose cry was almost indistinguishable from the baby's. Others have imitated the noise of the carpenters' saws and for a time we used to have one which reproduced the noise of a plane taking off at the airport thirty miles away and has

Married to Melanesia

several times deceived us into thinking that the airline schedules had been changed.

Driving into Honiara, we often see a megapod flapping clumsily across the road in the more uninhabited areas. We had been told that these birds were peculiar to the nearby small island of Savo, clearly visible across the sea from our road, but some must have been brought across in a canoe; one cannot imagine this bird flying so far. It is rather smaller than a domestic fowl but with very long legs and, as its name implies, enormous feet. It uses these feet for digging a deep hole in sandy ground in which it lays a single egg about twice the weight of an ordinary hen egg. It fills the hole in and goes away. The egg incubates itself without benefit of mother-bird and in due course hatches; then the megapod chick struggles up, three feet or more, to the surface. People watch these birds and learn their habits, for the eggs are often dug up and are much prized as food. Reuben, one of the Kohimarama labourers, evidently knows a spot in the bush where they are to be found and sometimes bring me one as a present. I now always look these gift-horses in the mouth; one fresh megapod egg makes a nice dish of scrambled eggs for the two of us but there is no way of knowing how old Reuben's finds are. I have not, however, had the experience of a friend in Honiara who was given an egg, put it down temporarily in a warm place in her kitchen and turned round to find a megapod bursting out of it.

Butterflies, unlike the parrots, are not shy but highly visible in the flowers immediately outside the house and I have never seen such huge and beautiful ones. Among the commonest is a beauty three or four inches across in black and brilliant turquoise blue. An even bigger one with delicate filigree wings in a subtle and elegant colour combination of brown and black is another frequent visitor. Unluckily, the butterflies are a very easy prey for the adolescent kittens we often have on the go and it is difficult to encourage ratting while discouraging butterfly collecting. The local children also have a deplorable

Beasts

butterfly game. They catch them, attach strings to their bodies and then fly them in competition with each other like kites.

Fish in our waters are colourful too and watching them from the jetty was one of our pleasures at Siota. The tank of local fish in the dining-room of the Mendana Hotel in Honiara never ceases to astonish me. One supposes that some biological reason for the extraordinary colours and shapes could be adduced but I can only think that God has a rich vein of fantasy in his nature which came out in the creation of tropical fishes, for fish, in other respects, are dullish things. Certainly some of these odd forms more nearly resemble a particularly outrageous Ascot hat than a creature with its living to get like the rest of us. Probably it is all on account of the coral which, heaven knows, comes in very strange shapes and colours and which is part of these fishes' habitat.

Turtles also form part of the marine scene and are highly thought of as food. This is very comprehensible, but the creatures always seem to suffer unnecessary agonies before they are butchered. They are tied up and flounder about, or are left lying helpless on their backs, often in the sun, in what seems to us a very callous manner. We once attended a feast at which an unfortunate turtle was present and alive throughout the proceedings till it was slaughtered at the end, cut into sections and distributed among the various villages represented. Its sufferings quite spoiled our feast, but perhaps we are unduly sensitive.

Apart from pigs, the main land animals seem to be rats which are a pest to everybody; one hears tales of them gnawing the soles of sleeping children's feet in village homes and even in some boarding schools. The answer to rats is undoubtedly cats, but these have suffered severely as a side effect of the World Health Organisation's malaria eradication programme. All buildings are regularly sprayed with DDT and the cats, catching insects and lizards from the walls as they will, have died in great numbers. Cats are therefore at a premium in the islands. Raymond Firth, the anthropologist, in one of his many

Married to Melanesia

books about the small island of Tikopia, tells how the Tikopians obtained their first cats from the even more remote island of Anuta, where cats were successfully controlling the rat population. 'Give us some of your long-tails', they are reported to have said, and a pair came over in a canoe. I was charmed by this story when I read it and promptly dubbed our Kate, who was a kitten at the time, a little long-tail. But whenever I have asked any of our – rather numerous – Tikopian students what their word for a cat is, they have invariably replied 'pussycat'. Indeed, 'pussycat' appears to be the word for a cat in every one of the seventy-three languages of the Solomons, as I was confounded to discover within weeks of my arrival when I was trying to make a linguistic point to an English class at Siota and went round the room asking the vernacular name of the first object to meet my eye, which happened to be a cat. The students present spoke about seven different languages among them and every man solemnly answered my question with the word 'pussycat'. My point went unmade.

Pussycats have certainly been among our dearest friends in our island homes, from Kate onwards. Poor Kate. She survived two ocean voyages, gave birth to a solitary kitten (claimed by David, named 'Siota', and given to his mother at Belaga as a parting present) but she was unable to tolerate the initial confusion of our life at Kohimarama. She was in kitten at the time and a houseful of builders banging in every corner obviously proved unendurable and she fled to the bush within a week or two of our arrival. I would not give much for her chances of survival. The Connors' Timid, on the other hand, survived and spent perhaps two years as the Kohimarama tomcat, going on occasional walkabout but always – until the last time – returning, dirty and hungry.

Our next kitten was another little tabby whom we named Min, partly after our favourite Goon and partly because she had a large M in black on her forehead. She was an exceptionally affectionate, purring creature who loved human company and would secrete herself in the spare room when there was a

Beasts

visitor with a view to appearing in the middle of the night, on or under the bed, purring loudly. Unfortunately, she came into season for the first time during one of Timid's absences, went off to look for a mate and was never seen again.

Min was one of a job lot of kittens given to Kohimarama by our neighbours at the Catholic secondary school seven miles away. They had been born and brought up on a beach under a coconut palm, which made their obvious love for human society the more remarkable. Min's sister went to the Bladeses, lived long and successfully and reared many a litter of healthy kittens, including a number of dazzlingly bright black cats, two of whom were adopted by our Canadian colleague and next-door neighbour, Paul Moore. These black twins, which he called Deacon and Sub-deacon, were known to us as Demon and Sub, or collectively, the Demons, which they patently were. They became our friends as we looked after them during their master's absences. As they grew up, they developed rather anxious, slightly neurotic personalities. If Paul was out for the day and later than usual in returning, the Demons would come to see us, very worried and plainly saying, 'He's gone away. We don't know where he is. What if he doesn't come back?' and after half an hour of this anxious cat-talk we would capitulate, go over to their house with them, break into their kitchen, open their fridge and find their 'Tucker Box' and feed them.

Timid by this time had departed on his final walkabout and the Connors, within a year of their own return to New Zealand, declared that they would not have another cat. But early one morning we were invaded by a large, ginger tomcat, handsome but no longer in his first youth, determined to live with somebody at Kohimarama and trying each house in turn. Ginger is the most persistent cat I have ever known and it was Nonie Connor he wore down in the end. We never knew where he came from, but he certainly knew what a fridge was for before he found out from the Connors. He settled down with them and became a worthy and formidable successor to Timid as the

Married to Melanesia

Kohimarama tom. He ate New Zealand style meals and became fat and well-liking.

Meanwhile, we had acquired the definitive cat of our island career, yet another little tabby, offspring of Min's sister, and we called her Jenny. As soon as she was adult – if not slightly before – she found an acceptable mate in Ginger and they have settled down as a sort of feline Darby and Joan. Jenny has kittens at intervals of approximately fifteen weeks and we are sometimes hard-pressed to dispose of the last of one family before the next family is born. We rather wish there was some kind of cat-contraceptive pill which could be used to regulate the output. We have thought of having her spayed, but both she and we enjoy the kittens. Besides, it is difficult to catch a vet at a convenient moment, as we found during the last kittening, when poor Jenny produced one kitten and, four hours later, still could not produce the rest and plainly expected me to do something about it. 'I suppose you've looked in the cat book?' said Eric. Of course I had, and of course it said, 'Call the vet.' So we bundled mother and baby into a basket and jolted off, at seven in the evening, to Honiara to see if we could find the government vet at his home – address unknown – and persuade him to help. The telephone book, when we got within reach of telephones, proved unhelpful, so we rang up the matron of the Central Hospital who had taken the last of the previous litter and asked her if she knew where the vet was. Yes indeed she did. He was flat on his back in the Central Hospital with a slipped disc. Why didn't we go and see him? Apologetically, we approached his bedside, taking turns to stay outside in the car with the cat, and asked his advice. He suggested all I could do was what *he* would do – scrub up my hands, vaseline my forefinger and have a poke around inside to see if I could get the next kitten into a suitable position to be born. So we jolted home, the little brute already born driving us and its mother crazy with its shrill cries, and I tried this crude midwifery, obviously causing extreme pain to a very patient cat, who bled a bit and then went out of labour and fell asleep, which was

Beasts

more than we could. Twenty-four hours later, out popped the other two and, after all this effort all were, for once, suffered to survive.

Ginger visits the house daily and is remarkably gentle with the kittens when they are of an age to play with his tail as he sits on the doorstep. Jenny will permit no other cat to come near, but Ginger is always welcome (if not by me) to a share of her food. The kittens are often remarkably handsome, tending to the white with a splodge of tabby or ginger. As a result of the rat problem and the DDT problem, we are always hearing of openings for enterprising young cats, but Eric has a tendency to say, 'They can't go out to work yet; they're too little', and we always seem to preserve from every litter a special favourite for whom we have to find a particularly good job. David is always eager to beg kittens for his friends and relations and we have now supplied the village of Belaga with two siblings of different generations. The first one, 'DK', was so named by David after the call-signal of the mission radio station at Taroaniara which says, 'DK calling, DK calling'. He became the favourite of his litter and David had to be given a week's holiday and his fare on a ship to take DK over to Gela for his mother (Siota had long since fallen victim to the DDT). There was also a family wedding at the time and the inevitable feast. David returned saying, 'I took some pudding for my pussy', so DK is all right at Belaga, getting his share of the feasts and of the catch when they go fishing. Margaret was said to be jealous because her grandmother had been given a cat and she had not got one, so we destined one of the next litter for her, a little she-cat called Coffee because of what looked like a few grains of instant coffee spilt on her white fur. The problem, as usual, was transport, until we heard at a few hours' notice of a diocesan ship going direct from Honiara to Belaga carrying building materials. We hastily packed Coffee into a basket, labelled her PUSSCAT FOR MARGARET BELAGA, packed a plastic carrier-bag with tins of milk, Tucker Box and an old saucer, labelled it RATIONS BELONG PUSSCAT, rushed into

Married to Melanesia

Honiara and confided the lot to the bos'n of the *Baddeley* and hoped for the best. We hear that DK and Coffee are now the cat heroes of Belaga, catching all their rats and fed indiscriminately by the entire village. We hope they will form an incestuous union and populate Gela with their kind. The value set on cats by village people can be guaged by a recent news item on the national radio programme. The people of Vuturua, a Gela village a few miles from Belaga, had just lost their only 'pussycat' (*sic* on the English language news). He was the only survivor of the DDT and was relied on by all the village as their rat-catcher, welcomed and fed in every house. On his death, the chief decreed a funeral feast. A pig was killed, fish were caught, puddings were made and the SIBS notified, all in honour of their departed pussycat. I felt an impulse to send them a replacement. It sounded almost as good a job as the one to which we had just sent our latest favourite kitten, at Government House no less, where the ADC had taken the opportunity to slip in a kitten in the brief interregnum between high commissioners, thus presenting the new incumbent with a *fait accompli*. We felt a little worried about the parquet floors and Persian carpets, watching the treatment our humbler vinyl and mats were suffering and inclined to say, 'Let the Queen look to her furnishings', but we hear he is a success. They have called him, for various reasons including his permanent costume of black dinner jacket and white shirt front, 'Bustopher Jones' and he will no doubt mature into a Cat About Town like his namesake in T. S. Eliot, growing portly off the rich pickings from all those gubernatorial dinner-parties.

Ginger lost his patrons the Connors, who went back to New Zealand, and had rather a thin time till the Tevis came into their house. I was hoping that the Tevis would take him on, so I kept him going in the interval, scrupulously feeding him not at our house but at his. As a result, he regards me as his patroness who might conceivably be intending to feed him at the end of any of my journeys about the compound, so he

Beasts

often accompanies me on academic trips, chirruping excitedly and expecting me to give his tail a friendly pull. The Tevis are good to him, but they are New Hebrideans and their life style does not include milk and cheese, so I often slip Ginger a dish of milk or some cheese rind outside our house to make him feel he is back with the New Zealanders.

All in all, we have a large circle of cat friends and rarely stir out of doors for a walk without an escort of Jenny or Ginger or an adolescent kitten or one or both of the Demons, though not usually all at once, for Ginger terrorises the neutered Demons and Jenny will only tolerate Ginger and members of her current family. Several earlier members of Jenny's family live in the immediate neighbourhood and remain our friends. They dare not come to the house as their mother spits at them, but they sometimes attend classes and one of them, a very gentle tabby tom known as the Bishop, is a special friend of Eric's, sitting on his study desk and helping with the administration and taking a particular interest in the teaching of Greek.

We have never kept a dog, being both cat people. Also, Jenny flies at any dog who comes near the house, much to our embarrassment if the harmless creature happens to be in the company of some visitor from Honiara who has driven him out for a country walk. Local dogs in general, however, it must be admitted, justify Jenny's darkest suspicions. They are kept for hunting, hardly fed at all and are really dangerous predators going about in packs at night and howling in the most eerie way. All the villages have such dogs and so do our neighbours, the Brothers. At one point, when the Brothers' dogs had been howling for half-hours on end on several successive nights, Eric was moved to protest to Head Brother. The Brothers discussed the matter among themselves and finally came up saying, 'We've decided what to do, Father. We're going to drive all the females away.' It seemed useless to protest and they presumably did what they had said. The only result was that a few months later we had a series of half-starved bitches returning from the bush to our compound –

Married to Melanesia

not the Brothers' – and having their puppies in all sorts of nooks and crannies. They were very wild and unapproachable. Luckily, one of the students at the time was an ex-police inspector who owned a (fully-licensed) gun and Simon was kept busy for a week or two despatching these poor brutes, after which we had to drown the puppies.

We have one legitimate Dog About the Place, Goldie, alias Wuff, a gentle labrador of uncertain age. He had had a number of European owners in Honiara, all of whom left the Protectorate, before he came into the family of Desmond Probets, the last English dean of the cathedral. When the Probetses left they gave Goldie to the Bladeses at Kohimarama. He settled well, took to a country life and particularly enjoyed escorting the children on their daily trips to swim in the river. But alas for Goldie. The Bladeses also departed for their native Australia at the same time as Ginger was deserted by the Connors, and Goldie was bequeathed to our friends at the Tanaemba Plantation, John and Margaret Vau, a middle-aged Melanesian couple. Goldie, we had already observed, suffered from colour prejudice and refused for many weeks to accept the Vaus as his patrons or the plantation manager's house as his home. We were in Australia ourselves at the time the Bladeses and the Connors left and it was embarrassing to come back to Ginger and Goldie, both of them convinced that happy days were here again and determined to live with me and be my love. Every time I drove on to the station, Goldie would run half a mile to greet me with humiliating ingratiation. He is a church-going dog and insisted on following me to church, lying beside me in the aisle, quietly trotting up behind me at the communion and totally ignoring the Vaus, who were usually present too. He refused to eat at the plantation and became pathetically thin. I fetched him bones from the butchery and gave them to Margaret Vau to feed to him. We repeatedly walked him home, paddling across the river *en route*, and giving him orders in the firm, authoritative English tones to which he would always respond.

Beasts

At last, when we were all thinking that the only recourse would be to Simon and his gun, the Vaus made a breakthrough and Goldie quite suddenly accepted them. We still see him often and he always greets us, but with dignity and not ingratiation. He is now Dog Vau and he knows his job, which is either to escort John around the plantation or Margaret, who is our nurse, to her morning and evening clinics and on her rounds in the student village. He still goes to church, but it is always John Vau he lies down beside.

Cows and goats are both very successfully kept on Guadalcanal but not by us. The students normally keep a pig fattening for the next feast and there are many discussions about its management, slaughter and replacement, with the appointment of a pig committee, a pig manager and so forth, but we do not visit it ourselves as it is destined for the ovens and we are squeamish. Goats we would rather like to keep, but we cannot really spare the land. We look with admiration at a large and multiplying herd on a plantation ten miles along the road to Honiara and wonder if they are milked. Probably not, as the kids run with their mothers, and indeed whole families, father and all, seem to run together. Some of the billies are truly patriarchal with their branching horns. I suppose they fight, but I have not seen them doing it.

One of the interests, indeed, of the local style of animal husbandry is the way the animal families do not seem to be separated. Cattle are now doing well in the Solomons. There seem to be few cattle diseases and no tsetse-fly and many of the islands are very well watered. The cattle graze under the coconut palms and on hot afternoons are to be seen standing in the numerous rivers cooling themselves, a picturesque, pre-industrial, pastoral scene. They are kept for meat and not, as yet, milked, so there are always young calves running about and also many great bulls which often stray into the road and look with potential truculence at oncoming vehicles. But I have never known them do any damage and they seem far less aggressive and dangerous than their English counterparts.

Married to Melanesia

Perhaps a placid family life with wives and children is better for their tempers.

We had a cow at Siota called Daisy. She had been imported by a previous warden and had, at one time, had a calf and given milk. There had also been, not too far away, a bull. But by the time we arrived, Daisy was the only representative of her kind on Small Gela. The calf had died and so had the bull whose owner, an agricultural assistant, had gone away temporarily and nobody had fed or watered the animal. All through our year at Siota Daisy was dry, lonely, and a very melancholy beast. The grass on the station was – so we were told – bad for cattle (they actually said poisonous, which I found hard to believe) and Daisy had to be hand-fed with kumara vines. She would occasionally come into season, break out of her fence, and roam about the station, looking in at our windows and lowing sadly. I never understood how she escaped forming a part of our final feast as we did not intend to ship her aboard the *Vonu*, but she was left alive and has subsequently, we hear, taken ship for Guadalcanal and joined a herd. She will, no doubt, have a very humble position in the pecking order in her new family, but anything would be better than her former melancholy solitude.

The only creatures we have actually kept for food have been hens. We immediately realised that this was the only reliable way of getting eggs; villagers would sell us eggs at Siota, but neither they nor we had any clear idea how old they were and during our first few months there were many horrid scenes in the kitchen when I broke egg after stinking egg. I eventually learned to make sure I had one good egg from my dozen *before* I committed myself to making a cake or a sweet.

We were both of us totally inexperienced chicken-keepers when we were given a scratch collection of half a dozen 'bush' hens of the local brown-to-black variety and took over an old run put up by one of our predecessors. Nonie Connor was our principal mentor at first and, over five years, we have learnt the rudiments, but not much more, of chicken management, im-

Beasts

porting pellets for them from Australia, feeding them in the morning, letting them out at teatime, shutting them in at dusk and making sure that they always have water. We have never deliberately kept a cock, but our ladies have persistently recruited a husband for themselves and one of these we tolerated for more than a year till we became convinced that he was a wife-murderer and killed him. He was just about as unpleasant after a couple of hours in the oven as he had been alive, though admittedly less noisy. Perhaps we should have followed, in his case, the practice of the French wife of a government officer who told us, as a serious culinary hint, that she fed brandy to fowls who were about to die. This relaxed their muscles (made them drunk to put it crudely) and made their flesh more tender. Gin was cheaper, she remarked, but she preferred brandy. Since she probably turned the happy birds into *coqs-aux-vin*, she may have been acting on the good old principle of never mixing the grain and the grape.

Our foolish hens never learn and they (or their successors; it is hard to think of them except as a collective – 'the hens') have made repeated attempts to have a cock-in-residence. They are rather like the poor little bride in the Book of Tobit whose bridegrooms never survived the wedding night, though, in that instance, on account of a demon. Whenever an aspiring cock is found on the roost, we let it be known among the families on the station that we have a trespasser who may be ransomed and shut up. If nobody claims him and removes him by the following Saturday, David kills him and has most of him for his own Sunday dinner, leaving me with a few scraps to make a chicken *creôle* for ours.

I never expected to enjoy hen-keeping – and indeed I could live without it – though I do enjoy egg-cooking. But the witless creatures have added their own small drop of entertainment to our beast-life. We have only once let a hen rear a brood. She hatched them under a bit of old iron-roofing by the warm copra-drier at Siota and it was fascinating to observe them grow up, gradually revealing their characteristics (mostly sex). But

Married to Melanesia

as a species they are not sufficiently individual and they just are not clever enough or amusing enough. When I think of hens, I think of interminable evenings at the time we moved their house and of myself patrolling the place like a goosegirl with a long bamboo stick, shepherding the stupid creatures into their new house and fending them off the old one. Or the nights when we have been in bed and the evening electricity finished and one of us has remembered to wonder 'Did we shut those birds in?' and Eric has stumbled out with a torch to make sure. We never forget the night when the Brothers' dogs got into the Connors' hen-run, soon after their return from leave when they were starting a new flock of expensive, imported young chicks, and killed the lot before George, hearing the hullabaloo, could get out of bed and find a stick to beat them off.

When I am an urban housewife again, buying my eggs in the supermarket, I have no doubt it will take me some time to stop waking up at night wondering if all is well, or to break the association of teatime with hentime, which has become part of the rhythm of our daily life. But I shall be quite happy to pay somebody else to produce the eggs.

XI

BOTANICAL

Farmers in the tropics tend to have gardens rather than farms, smallish pieces of ground that can be cultivated with simple hand tools and do not need machinery. *The* tool in the Solomon Islands is the bush knife, a stout, fairly thick blade some two feet long and two inches wide with a handle. This is part of the personal equipment of any adult of either sex (indeed children graduate to wielding it when alarmingly young) and country people rarely move about without one, so that anybody on the roadside to whom one gives a lift is generally brandishing a large knife. This need cause no alarm, except for the upholstery of the car.

These knives are very versatile. They will cut grass and tangled weeds and slash one's path through the bush; they will chop down all but the biggest and toughest trees; they will split open coconuts; they will decapitate big fish; they are also used, mainly by women, for the sort of detailed weeding and planting out in a flower garden which I do with little forks and trowels.

Here, as in Africa, the typical garden, as opposed to 'plantation' which is on a bigger scale and involves machinery, is a confused mixture and the ignorant European newcomer, looking at it, may not even immediately recognise it as cultivated ground at all, especially if an untidy crop such as kumara or cassava predominates. In the Solomons, there will certainly be coconut palms, sometimes there will be cocoa underneath, here a few banana trees, there a patch of pineapples, a few chilli bushes, cassava where nothing else will grow, kumara, and

113

Married to Melanesia

usually a good many weeds and creepers masking the total effect. By the time I reached the Pacific I was well accustomed to this style of cultivation and not expecting to see meadows or cornfields or even turnip fields all tidily demarcated with hedges or fences. Nor was I expecting wild nature to provide a riot of colour, having got over my disappointment, years earlier in Africa, at seeing altogether too much sun-baked earth and dried up brown grass and finding the tropical forests gloomy rather than vivid and their wild flowers rather small and insignificant against the overwhelming green.

So it was a pleasure to find the Solomons, at first blush, looking more like the tropical paradises of the travel brochures. The plentiful rain keeps the grass remarkably green most of the year round, and things do grow easily. Moreover the village people, unlike Africans for the most part in my experience, really do seem to love flowers and most villages are gay with hibiscus and other flowering shrubs. People – men even more than women and children – will pick a hibiscus flower as they go about their daily work and stick it in their hair. On washing days I often notice David with a flower behind one ear to balance the cigarette behind the other, the presence of both forgotten. He has casually picked one of the blindingly-red blooms off the hibiscus bush by the back door on his way to the clothes line.

On festive occasions, people hang themselves about with all sorts of vegetation, notably hats and crowns of twisted palm fronds and wreaths of wild vines round their necks and heads, all garnished with half a dozen hibiscus blooms. This is not so much on the festival day itself as during the hard-working period of preparation beforehand. These decorations give an oddly Bacchanalian look to a very sober people (unlike Polynesians, Melanesians do not make any kind of alcoholic drink) but obviously for them they are an expression of festal feeling.

The coconut palm frond is the real basis of all decoration whether of the person or of places. The leaves are shredded into a fringe and then they dry yellowish-brown and the result

Botanical

can be turned into a grass skirt for dancing or hung about a building, or on a shelter used for watching dancing – or even draped round a war relic, such as an old tank or a wrecked aircraft, when tourists are expected. I find the effect rather tatty myself but it clearly stimulates festal feelings in Solomon Islanders. Churches on the major festivals are apt to become impenetratable mazes of this stuff. During the Easter season one year we went to a service in Marovovo School chapel along the coast and found ourselves penned by coconut curtains into small oblong cubicles. You could see nothing of what was going on and it was impossible to stand or kneel without getting entangled in a sort of tickly grass skirt at head and shoulder level. The procession of clergy and servers nearly broke their necks dodging the hazards.

'Doing the church flowers' is one of the few of those activities beloved of pious ladies everywhere that I actually enjoy, but I have never meddled with it here because I can see that I am a stranger to the Pacific conventions of beauty. On ordinary Sundays, two baskets of, often strangely assorted, flowers are provided on the altar – no water – and reappear on the breakfast table at the community meal which follows the service. On festivals, there are some very tortured arrangements indeed which traditionally go with the church's 'grass skirts'. These take a lot of time and patience to prepare and only last for twenty-four hours or less. Solomon Islanders would appreciate the Derbyshire well-dressing, which is an equally transient art form and requires an equal amount of patient fiddling; it is their sort of thing. Here, people will take fresh palm fronds, arrange them in a cross or a triangle and spike a single flower – often of frangipani – on the end of each long leaf. Sometimes, particularly at Easter, hibiscus buds are used. There is a great art in selecting the right buds; they must be tomorrow's flowers, picked overnight (a hibiscus flower lasts just one day). With a bit of luck the flowers come out during the service, starting at dawn as tight, dark blobs and flashing out in brilliant red or yellow or pink by the end of the service when the sun

Married to Melanesia

is fully up. The glory is all over by evening and Easter Monday is a rather bedraggled and faded aftermath.

The only time I ever let myself go with flowers – outside the house, that is – was one Whit Sunday when Reuben, a New Hebridean student, was married in the college chapel. Ruth, his bride, is a tall, striking-looking girl, unlike most of the Solomon Islands girls who tend to be small and round. She had flown up from the New Hebrides and had brought with her a white lace, European-style bridal gown, which she had made herself. Reuben wanted her to wear 'something on her head' to go with it (Melanesian women normally go bareheaded) and applied to me. I was puzzled, but eventually contrived a bridal veil out of a white net curtain, surmounted by an enormous double pink hibiscus flower from our front garden. The enterprise went to *my* head and I was up well before dawn on the wedding day prowling the garden in my dressing gown with a pressure lamp, constructing bouquets for the bride, bridesmaids and 'olgeta'. Naturally, I left the church decorations to the young men who did the thing in style – their own style. I do not think I have ever seen a prettier wedding party or a more elegant bridal veil, thanks largely to the ever-beautiful and ubiquitous, if highly evanescent, hibiscus.

Hibiscus bushes and hedges, although the commonest of shrubs, are, to my mind, the most attractive of our garden plants and I have established a number of new varieties in our garden. They grow very easily, and sometimes by accident, from cuttings. Indeed, many things grow with embarrassing ease. One pushes an apparently dead bit of wood into the ground for some purpose, turns one's back and ends up with a forest, or at least a grove. Our hens live in the lavish shelter of a leafy bower which has spontaneously developed from the timbers which support the chicken wire of their run. As for our clothes post, it is known as Aaron's Rod and is a positive tree under which we sometimes park the car for shade. It started as a stout piece of wood from the bush for supporting one end of the clothes line and now it has to be regularly lopped.

Botanical

The garden trees abound in epiphytes (not parasites; they grow on the tree but get their nourishment independently from the air and the rain and the dust) of all kinds, the most attractive of which are the tree orchids which we certainly did not set and I doubt if anybody else did. Their seeds must be, like freedom, blowing in the wind, for I even found orchids had taken hold on the unprepossessing concrete of the water tank. Regretfully, I had to tear them off as we cannot afford to destroy or weaken the tank.

My attitude to gardens is very much that of the village cultivator. None of my tropical gardens has been planned; they always consist of whatever will grow from casual cuttings and seeds scrounged from here and there. One of my most successful crops of flowers, some brilliant petunias, came to my Ghana garden from some seed-heads I idly broke off and dropped into my handkerchief in a Kentish convent garden a day or two before my return to Africa one September. I have never made pedantic distinctions between the useful and the ornamental. We regularly have volunteer tomatoes under our sitting-room windows at Kohimarama (though I have not noticed either us or our guests spitting out seeds that way) and I let them grow with the roses and the bougainvillea and produce the odd fruit if they like. And I remember a year in Ghana when my front door was wreathed, all one wet season, in a splendid vine which had spontaneously developed from grape pips which really had been spat out; it never produced grapes alas – the original ones were imported. I was tempted to plant a fig biscuit on the other side in the hope of sitting, like the biblical patriarchs, in a state of eschatological peace under my own vine and my own fig tree, none making me afraid.

I am not, in fact, a serious cultivator of vegetables. I meant to try when we first came to Kohimarama because conditions are favourable, but all our village neighbours are so much better at it than I am that I do not like to compete. In marked contrast with Siota, 'ravens' abound at the front door, bearing a regular supply of French beans, Chinese cabbage, tomatoes,

Married to Melanesia

green peppers, pawpaws, bananas, sometimes a pumpkin and water melons and pineapples in their season. We found mango and soursop trees already in the garden, but, as I have already mentioned, we fight a losing battle with the flying-foxes for possession of the fruit. I have planted orange, lemon and mandarin trees for our successors and they are doing well. All citrus seem to do well here, but, with the exception of some excellent limes, they are regarded by the local people as exotics. We have been less lucky than most people with pawpaws. These come in trees of either sex and a remarkably high proportion of our seedlings turn out to be males on reaching maturity. But we persevere and, after several years, have our own pawpaws on the breakfast table. The pineapples 'down by the hens' on the other hand look remarkably promising and I am always surprised that we so rarely seem to eat them. I am not without my suspicions that I have *bought* my own pineapples at the front door.

One thing I am a sucker for is packets of flower seeds. Hope springs eternal and I buy dollar after dollarworth of these gaily-coloured promises of beauty every time they appear off a New Zealand ship in the Honiara stores. I have a failure rate of at least 90 per cent, possibly because I just fling the seeds in among the general floral chaos and let them fight it out with their neighbours, but anything rare which does come into bloom is sure of an admiring audience of students' wives and its seed heads are carefully garnered and often taken to other islands. Many temperate climate summer flowers seem to be a failure in the tropics, not so much, I suspect, because of the temperature, but perhaps because they are 'long-day' creatures. This should mean that the equinoctial-flowering plants could do well and I certainly have had a modest success with small chrysanthemums, a plant whose exacting demands in the matter of daylight – so much and no more – was imprinted on my memory by a curious English case I once read in a *Times* law report. A tenant on a municipal housing estate was a grower of champion class chrysanthemums. The Council installed day-

Botanical

light-style street lighting along the road he lived on, and left it on all night. The chrysanthemums – 'short-day' flowers – were fooled into thinking it was perpetual summer-with-Northern-lights and refused to produce their usual September glories. The grower sued the Council and I think he won his case, but I do not expect they switched off the lights at half past six every evening for the comfort of the flowers.

Spring flowers – presumably 'short-day' too – are simply not on in the tropics; it is too hot. But we do have numerous lilies, notably a splendid, large, upstanding orange beauty which surrounds our house having been planted round the old chapel next door and multiplied exceedingly. These only flower once a year, but they go on flowering for two months or more and they provide me with my best and most long-lasting cut flowers for the house. They are not unlike large daffodils, apart from their dazzling orange colour. Less satisfying but more spectacular is an enormous and heavily-scented white lily, clumps of which I have established under the spare bedroom window. It has outbursts of glory every few months, but only for twenty-four hours at a time. What looks very much more like a spring flower is the zephyranthe lily, which we used to call rain flowers in Ghana and which bloom regardless of season after a downpour of rain has brought an end to a dry period; they look just like purple crocuses. I have made borders of these all round the bit of garden just outside the front door and they too multiply vigorously. The kittens, unfortunately, find their leaves kitten-forest size and play and hunt and roll in them, so that they tend to be a bit bedraggled during the frequent kitten-toddler seasons.

At certain times after rain, the whole compound comes out in a rash of tiny mushrooms. I was emboldened by Nonie Connor's example to eat these. They were delicious and we did not die. Successive waves of building are engulfing the mushroom grounds but the local people, astonished to see me gathering these negligible blobs, have taken to bringing me the 'bush' mushrooms which grow on the rotting roots of old

Married to Melanesia

sago-palms. A 'mushroom raven' – usually a child – is always greeted with rapture and the menu quickly adjusted to accommodate twenty cents worth (sometimes as much as 2 lb) of enormous fungi at the very next meal. I cook them *à la Provençale* in butter with a soupçon of garlic and a dash of tarragon, turn some of my home-made brown bread into garlic toast to eat with them and we sit down to a gourmet meal, thanking God for the 'ravens' of Guadalcanal and the gas stove as we look back on the early Robinson Crusoe days with the tin-opener at Siota.

Kapok trees are among the things we are well blessed with at Kohimarama. They were presumably planted many years ago by the catechist students at St Andrew's and they are now fully mature. Indeed, some of them are rather elderly and in danger of collapsing, which they rather easily do especially in a cyclone, and we have had, most regretfully, to cut one down behind our kitchen lest it fall on the house. There are plenty left, however, and they are pretty things, tall, with rather pale green leaves, slightly feathery, and standing out elegantly against a clear blue sky. Their fruiting season comes in October to November, when the brown seed pods, six or seven inches long, spontaneously explode and spread the small black seeds cocooned in white wool all around, the fluff blowing about in the wind and reminding me of my Lancashire childhood when bits of loose cotton used to fly off bales on the back of lorries and we children would catch and collect it and play with it.

The Ghanaians call this stuff 'silk cotton' but I have never heard the Melanesians refer to it except as kapok. They value it highly for stuffing cushions and pillows – these are among the standard items in all our local fund-raising bazaars – and of course people want it for their own use. They prefer to 'shoot' the pods down from the trees with stones before they burst and scatter the 'cotton'. There always seems a lot of competition and jealousy in the kapok fruiting season. David will go off duty at the weekend straitly charging me to watch 'our' trees and chase off any predatory students or villagers. I gener-

Botanical

ally end up finding him a bit of 'calico' as well and stitching a pillow-case or two on my sewing machine for the reception of 'our' – to wit David's – kapok.

The students grow as many of their own vegetables as we have the land for, especially the staple root, kumara. Coconuts are another staple and though the compound is full of them we never have enough. They are mostly used for cooking in the form of milk, the nuts being first grated and then squeezed through a sieve with water. If the milk is left to stand, coconut cream can be skimmed off and this is delicious. We sometimes use it in a Polynesian dish, kokoda, which consists of raw white fish, marinated overnight in neat lime juice, then washed and slightly salted and covered in coconut cream.

Some of my coconut milk recipes are mild curries from south India, requiring not curry powder but ginger and turmeric. Turmeric grows in the Solomons – the Tikopians have grown it for years but, as far as I know, they have only used it for painting their bodies – and the Agricultural Department is currently promoting it as a cash crop, but I have never been able to get hold of a root and I do not know how to dry and process it if I grew it, so I go on resentfully paying seventy cents for a little tin of turmeric powder processed in Australia. Ginger, on the other hand, flourishes on the premises, 'in the back, down by the hens' and when I embark on a south Indian *moly* I send David out to 'shoot' down a coconut and grub up a root of ginger. This gives me a most satisfactory feeling of living off the land. David regards my proceedings as eccentric. His people know ginger, he says darkly, but as a medicine not food. I refrain from asking what it is supposed to do, suspecting it is an aphrodisiac.

There used to be an incense tree hard by the ginger which had been planted, we think, in association with the original church site for a convenient supply of incense. Unluckily, the students – pyromaniacs to a man – accidentally burned it down. They were clearing land for gardens and the fire got out of hand and took fierce hold on this very oily tree. It was a great

Married to Melanesia

sight, a pillar of fire by night and of smoke by day and it produced a delicious smell, smouldering on for many days. But we were sorry, and rather angry, about its fate; it was a beautiful tree and wantonly destroyed.

It is an astonishing thing that Solomon Islanders go on using fire with such gay abandon since even now, more than thirty years after the Battle of Guadalcanal, the bush is still littered with unexploded bombs, shells and hand grenades. In the middle of Honiara itself a man lit a bonfire recently at the foot of a tree in his front garden and set off a bomb which blew in the windows of the deanery next door and nearly blew up a passer-by in the road. In our country district we are always hearing explosions in the middle distance as people burn off land for new gardens. The Government is employing a British army expert to deal with the more obvious of the known hazards and it is only two or three years since he defused and removed a 500 lb bomb which had been sitting since 1942 outside the main dormitory at Marovovo School twelve miles along the coast from us.

So we are nervous when the students start a new agricultural push in case they should blow themselves up or burn the place down, but the most we have yet had to cope with has been the emergency evacuation of the hens before smoke and flames.

XII

'IN JOURNEYINGS OFT . . .'

About half-way through our year at Siota I went across to Honiara on some business or other and came back with the shopping a few days later. I had travelled as far as Taroaniara on a diocesan ship and spent the night there, sending a radio message to Siota asking them to send the 'speedboat' down the Passage to fetch me. (We listened daily at Siota on our transistor radio to the 'sked', the mission's scheduled half-hour of messages, but we had no transmitter and so could never reply to anything that was said to us.) Next morning there was no sign of the 'speedboat' so the Taroaniara people offered to send me home in the *Hilda*, their run-about boat, open to the heavens, no deck, with a central engine that you had to keep your legs out of. I was thankful to accept and also, in a way, thankful that it was pouring with rain which meant that I would only get soaked and not frizzled by the sun. They even lent me a raincoat. We put my suitcase and three months' shopping (for ourselves and others) in the bottom of the boat, covering it sketchily with a piece of plastic, and embarked, but we had not gone more than a couple of miles before we met the 'speedboat' in the middle of Port Purvis, the place where the Boli Passage broadens out to a width of three miles or so. A student was driving it and, to my surprise, Eric was sitting huddled in the bows under an umbrella wearing oilskins and clutching a small suitcase.

Port Purvis was a comfortable sheltered harbour for the

Married to Melanesia

massed American Fleet during the Battle of the Coral Sea in 1942, but we were not in destroyers and it did feel a bit exposed for two small boats in a high wind and a deluge. However, we contrived to stop alongside each other and cling on to the respective boats while we parleyed. Eric was unexpectedly having to go to Honiara to deal with some emergency and would be away a few days. Had not we better swop boats? So he climbed aboard the *Hilda* and I perilously lowered myself into the 'speedboat'. We transferred the cargo and then we swopped raincoats, a pretty useless operation as we were both soaking wet already, said goodbye and went our several ways. An hour later I was scrambling ashore on the Siota beach and the students were seizing the sodden cargo to carry it up to the house. I remember that it included a boxful of beer. The bottom fell out and the bottles scattered in all directions, but fortunately on the soft sand which did not break them. Wading ashore with the shopping, I reflected that my career as a housewife had started rather late in life and my shopping trips were taking a somewhat unusual form for a middle-aged clergyman's wife.

We never quite got used to that stretch of sea, nor to the ships which crossed it. The *Baddeley* and the *Selwyn* were the two work-horses of the diocese, carrying people and stores and building materials round from island to island, and we could usually get on one of them if we went to Taroaniara. They were uncomfortable but tolerable for the distance involved, unless one was ill. Most missionaries seemed to take them in their stride and travel vast distances in them. Neither of them had so much as a lavatory until Miss Lily Best, an Englishwoman even older than us, ex-WREN, of aristocratic background and accustomed to speaking her mind, came to make film-strips for the diocese. She was outraged by a number of things and said so. One of the small reforms she managed to institute was the provision of a loo on the *Baddeley* and another on the *Selwyn*, loudly proclaiming her refusal to sail on 'looless luggers'. But this was after we were safely on dry

'In Journeyings Oft . . .'

land on Guadalcanal and no longer at the mercy of diocesan shipping.

The *Hilda* was a really evil little boat. She was unbelievably noisy, she stank of diesel oil and one had to perch carefully on her sides trying not to fall either into the sea or the engine and, if possible, not to be sick. The *Hilda* terrified our kitten, Kate, when we first brought her home to Siota, and no wonder. She finally sank, I imagine unlamented, during a cyclone in 1972 and one hopes the insurance was put towards something more serviceable.

Sometimes we travelled from Taroaniara to Siota on the *Ara ni Ulu*, a 'cutter-boat' belonging to a co-operative society which had put her into the mission's boat yard for repairs and failed to pay for the work. ('Cutter-boat' is the local generic term for any small ship with a hold and a deck and a cabin and an engine.) The *Ara ni Ulu* must have been the slowest ship in the Pacific. If the tide was running against her she had difficulty in standing still, let alone moving forward, and her bos'n, Gordon, was an old man of an excessively cautious disposition who feared to overstrain the engine. On one occasion we were attending a feast at the girls' school on the small island of Bunana, just off Gela. Bishop Dudley Tuti was the guest of honour. We were going on to Honiara on the *Southern Cross*, but the Bishop was due at a conference at the other end of Gela and the *Ara ni Ulu* was sent over from Taroaniara to take him there. He was carried on board with some pomp, garlanded, and we all stood respectfully on the beach waving him goodbye, the schoolgirls singing farewell songs. The *Southern Cross* was riding at anchor waiting for the Bishop to depart. The *Ara ni Ulu*'s engines started up and the ship moved ten yards out into the current to the cheers of the girls, but there she stood, puffing but quite stationary, for an embarrassing half-hour. But at least the *Ara ni Ulu* had an awning and she did not smell, so a long, idle afternoon could be spent not disagreeably on her deck, drifting down the Boli Passage.

One of the reasons why we particularly looked forward to

Married to Melanesia

moving to Guadalcanal was the road. We would treat ourselves to a vehicle, we thought, and become mobile and self-propelled. The road really called for a Land-Rover we were told, but we could not afford that and, months before we moved, we ordered ourselves a Mini-Moke. They were cheap and they had an air of determination and no-nonsense sturdiness, so we hoped this poor man's substitute would serve. As soon as the road was passable after our arrival at Kohimarama, I contrived to get myself to Honiara and went to demand my Moke. But the agent knew nothing about us; the man we had seen had returned to Australia in a hurry (and perhaps under a cloud), the orders were in a frightful mess and, in short, we would have to start again. While I was thinking this over, I saw outside the rival garage a row of small Japanese pick-ups just unloaded from a ship. We were desperate for transport (the college did not acquire its truck until several months later), so I went in to enquire, was taken for a trial run and returned home in triumph behind the wheel, presenting Eric with a *fait accompli*. Luckily, he was pleased.

Our little truck had a cab big enough for two people and an open platform behind, which would take a legal maximum of eight passengers and often had to, though this weight grossly overloaded the two-stroke engine. The students lined the floor with a sort of trampoline of sago-palm trunks, the material used for kneeling on in village churches, and this did something to mitigate the discomfort of squatting on the back. After waiting for a few months for another ship from Japan, the truck was fixed up with a 'house', as the students put it, and this kept passengers and cargo moderately dry in wet weather; but journeys were always uncomfortable, what with the sun and the dust and the jolting.

We practically drove the little truck into the ground in eight or nine months. It carried water from the river for our houses. It carried sacks of rice and flour. It carried drums of diesel and petrol and it carried innumerable people in all sorts of emergencies, usually to hospital. If a woman was about to 'deliver',

'In Journeyings Oft . . .'

twenty-five miles on our truck was enough to bring the baby on, at speed. The truck saw both the beginning and the end of life for on one occasion it carried a corpse away from the hospital. Eric had driven himself one morning – *per miraculum* alone – to see the doctor because he felt ill. It was pouring with rain and, as he came away from the hospital he met our friend the dean of Honiara who greeted him as a dispensation of providence because he had a corpse on his hands – an Anglican corpse – to be got back, if possible, to a village well beyond Kohimarama, in fact beyond the end of the road, for burial. It was a young woman who had died in childbirth. The husband was with her and an older child. Could Eric help? What can you do in such circumstances? They lifted the body, wrapped in a mat, on board and set off. They drove to the end of the road and there Eric left them waiting for people to be assembled to carry the body on through the bush to the village. When he did not return by lunchtime I was beginning to conclude that he was so ill that he had been admitted to hospital, but about two o'clock he turned up, rather worse in health than he had started out and very wet, with a bottle of pills and this story of a body.

When at last the college was given a two-ton truck we felt that the little pick-up had more than done its job and we traded it in for a car, surprised that anyone would buy it. The car was a nice little job, also Japanese, and slightly more powerful than the truck. But, as with the truck, the puncture rate was high and also the starter motor happened to be rather low-slung, constantly filled up with water in the rivers and regularly packed up. We kept this vehicle for a year, at the end of which we went on leave to Australia but not before we had cast covetous eyes on the first Mazda coupé to reach the Solomons. It was a beautiful car, sleek and streamlined and obviously comfortable (at least it would be on any normal road), in a rich Oxford blue and we fell for the sales talk, which included an offer to sell it to us complete with extras such as a radio, at the basic price. We also calculated – accurately as it turned out –

Married to Melanesia

what the yen was likely to do in the next few months and decided that it would be advantageous to buy then and not later. Thus it came about that we went off to Australia leaving behind us two cars, one of them deplorably unmissionary – even unclerical – and decidedly unmiddle-aged. We have – at vast expense and trouble – cherished it and intend to send it home when we go. Having got it to England we shall restore its floor coverings, wheel-trims, etc. (unusable here because of the rivers), switch the radio on to the BBC and, petrol supplies permitting, whizz up and down the M6 in it, which will be a surprise for it as it has never had a chance to do 60 mph in its life.

Twenty-three miles to Honiara post office does not, perhaps, sound much, but Guadalcanal is well watered and the road crosses many rivers. Some of them, at the Honiara end, are bridged. Many are quite minor, reduced to a trickle in the dry season, and flow over a concrete ford. The Tanaemba, the Sasaa and the Umasani are quite big however and always fairly full of water, and we cross them on the pebbles and boulders without benefit of concrete. The Umasani used to have a 'low-level' bridge, a sort of concrete causeway just under normal water level, but this was swept away in the floods of early 1971 and has never been replaced in spite of much political agitation. It is the longest of our rivers and rises relatively slowly but when it is up it stays up, sometimes for weeks on end, and can effectually cut us off from Honiara. The Sasaa was never bridged. It is a picturesque and excitable little river, quickly up and down and always changing course; it has rather steep banks down which one gently lowers one's vehicle into a very stony bed, full of great boulders which the Public Works Department occasionally sends a monster to nudge aside. The rule with the Sasaa is 'Never cross it when it is running brown.' A neighbour of ours once tried to do so in a quite heavy station waggon. She narrowly escaped with her life and the vehicle was swept downstream practically into the nearby sea and totally wrecked. The Tanaemba is our local river. Not content with

'In Journeyings Oft . . .'

having a bridge over it just where our side road comes out into the main road (it was this bridge which was down the first few weeks we were at Kohimarama), it perversely divides and gives rise to yet another ford, normally quite shallow but capable of filling up with roaring water. Our builders are in the habit of setting up their concrete-block making machine by the road at this point and recently had it all swept away in a sudden downpour in the middle of the dry season. It was lost for several days, but after prolonged search in the bush they recovered it when the waters receded.

All these rivers are apt to change course suddenly, which is one reason why they are not bridged. The ultimate bridging will be a major engineering job and when we ask about it we are told, 'It is in the Development Plan.' A few miles farther out from Honiara than us, a small tourist resort has been set up. Tourists, mostly American and often elderly, come out for a romantic night in the bush – no electricity but otherwise comfortable – and it is their adventures with the rivers rather than our run-of-the-mill ones which get into the news reports on the radio. They sometimes have a more romantic experience than they had bargained for in getting back to their aeroplanes if it happens to have been a very wet night.

The surface of the road is profitable for tyre manufacturers, being largely stones and loose gravel, but the PWD do their best with it with a grader, except during the long close season for graders when the incessant rain makes their labours rather more than usually like those of Sisyphus. Driving along, one is choked with dust in the dry weather and apt to skid on patches of mud in wet weather, but it is a *road* and therefore a rarity in the Solomons and, in spite of all its drawbacks we are, looking back on our marooned condition at Siota, truly grateful for it.

The journey into Honiara is, if one were less preoccupied by cares than we usually are when we make it, a singularly beautiful drive. To the left the sea is always visible, sometimes within a few yards of the road, and it varies in colour from a leaden grey to a most lovely turquoise blue. Usually calm in the

Road to Honiara

'In Journeyings Oft ...'

mornings, it is often whipped up by a wind around noon and full of white horses, sparkling in the sun, all afternoon. The small island of Savo five miles off shore lies there like a sea-slug or, to some fantasies, like Queen Victoria lying in state. The Gela mountain peaks, thirty or forty miles off, can be seen if the weather is at all clear. The road runs through a series of plantations, green down to the shore line, coconut palms (some of the older ones bearing shrapnel holes from the fighting in 1942) gracefully waving, sleek cattle with many calves grazing below. To the right, a few miles inland, are the mountains of Guadalcanal, almost as varied as the sea, clearly outlined and classical against an intensely blue sky on many a hot morning – very Greek – but often in the afternoons heavy with black rain clouds. After rain, as the cloud rises, the sky and all the air seem washed and wisps of cloud hang about the lower levels of the mountains and I always think how like Westmorland it looks and feel homesick. The rivers, admittedly a constant anxiety, are in themselves the most beautiful tropical rivers I have ever known, clear, fast-flowing over stones and between trees, their mountain origins plainly visible. I do actually love them at night, especially at full moon, when one gently launches the car into the water, scarcely able to see the opposite bank, and drives softly across in bottom gear watching the little fishes leaping in the moonlight and the headlights and hearing the frogs at their everlasting song.

In the opposite direction from Honiara, we often have to drive out to Marovovo School on the rocky end of Guadalcanal. Turning south beyond the school, the road climbs over the mountainous west end of the island – the place where, in pagan 'custom' belief, the spirits of the dead take off into the sunset, a beautiful and rather eerie spot, descending suddenly to a beach with a reef which is the nearest satisfactory fishing ground to Kohimarama and where we always have to drive the students for a ritual night's fishing on the eve of any feast. Our journeys are often anxious but always beautiful.

The two-ton truck has been invaluable. It will take thirty-two

Married to Melanesia

passengers or a fair quantity of cargo. It will also manage to cross the rivers when smaller vehicles cannot, though there are times when even the truck cannot reach Honiara and there have been occasions when it and its passengers have been caught on the wrong side by a sudden rise in the rivers that has happened since they set out. One of the concrete fords quite near home is known to us as George's Creek in memory of the time when George Connor took a truckload of students into Honiara, including wives and small children, and was stopped at this point on his way home by a rushing torrent. There was nothing to do but wait the night till the floods receded. I have only twice in four years seen any water at all in George's Creek.

During the rainy season between Christmas and Easter we expect the road to be out of action quite often, even if there are no cyclones and no bridges are actually swept away; if that happens, it is simply closed for longer. We always keep stocks of food so that the whole community can manage for several weeks without shopping, but medical emergencies can be trying and we often feel the lack of a telephone. One year, we had a new member of staff with his wife and two children arriving on the same day in February as Jim and Elizabeth Blades and their three children were due back from leave. A downpour supervened, the rivers rose, and it was quite impossible for anybody to go and meet them. A week passed before they could be fetched by truck, or indeed communicated with at all and we wondered what the newcomers must think of their new abode. We are always nervous when we have overseas visitors during the rains as we can never be sure of being able to get them back to their aeroplanes on the right day.

To Melanesians, the solution is obvious; use the sea. This is what we did ourselves when we came back from leave in 1972 on the day after a cyclone which had done a great deal of damage and, as a minor effect, swept a few bridges away and put our road out of commission for weeks. The Bishop said we must have the *Southern Cross* to get us along the coast so

'In Journeyings Oft . . .'

we thought hastily and visited the bank and the shops to set ourselves up for a siege. I had, in three months away from home forgotten what was in the house, but we bought the usual sacks of rice and sugar, a bit of fresh food, a carton of beer and some torch batteries. We even remembered that the community store might have run short of local tobacco, a state of affairs which depresses morale almost more than anything else, so we took a supply of that on board too and suffered a very smelly night with it in our cabin. We were still wearing our respectable going-on-leave clothes, so our descent over the side into the ship's dinghy and subsequent wading ashore, clutching overcoats and cameras and suitcases and Sydney Airport's smart 'duty-free' carrier bags, must have presented rather a curious spectacle on the beach opposite 'Harrods'. We have lately been considering ordering an outsize canoe with an outboard motor (canoes are made which will take thirty or forty men). It would be slower than the truck but it would get there – and could take fishing parties out on to the reef, or football teams, the sick, shopping parties, and so on into Honiara. And it would be an all-weather form of transport.

We very rarely make a trip on purely private business or pleasure as there are always people who really need to go to Honiara, even to the point where there is sometimes not enough room for both of us in our own car. If we do plan a pleasure excursion, especially at night, something is sure to go wrong. The first evening we were invited out after our arrival at Kohimarama was to a drinks party given by our bank to celebrate the opening of its new building. We thought it might be fun – after the rusticities of Siota – to dress up and go out, so we prepared to set off in our little truck. We climbed in and started the engine but the truck refused to budge out of the garage. We got out and pushed, but the wheels would not turn round. (Later, we got used to this. The brakes often seized up as a result of being sodden in the rivers and we learned how to deal with them.) The large diocesan truck happened to be on the place having delivered stores and was about to return

Married to Melanesia

empty to Honiara, so the students lifted the little vehicle bodily on to the back and we waved it and our cocktail party goodbye and went back into the house to remove our finery.

The rivers seem to know when any of us are planning an evening out in Honiara. Our new Australian colleagues, John and Sharon Pinson, were delighted to be invited, early in their Melanesian career, to a drinks party at Government House to celebrate Australia Day. It happened to be Sharon's birthday and they planned to eat out afterwards. They equipped their children with a baby-sitter, took John's best suit out of mothballs and aired it in the sun and at five o'clock, dressed by our standards to the nines, they climbed into their Moke and set out for the party. Alas, they got no farther than the Tanaemba ford at the bottom of our own road. A freak storm in the hills had swelled the river and their engine stalled midstream and could not be restarted. They did not want to ruin their clothes, so John took his suit off and Sharon her dress and they jumped out, barefoot and in their pants, to push the car to the bank – and were slightly embarrassed to be caught in this posture by the labourers from the plantation who appeared, at this point, to help.

We did not actually drive into the Sasaa but prudently turned back on the night – also in the 'dry' season – when we had tickets for the Honiara amateur dramatic society's play and had invited Paul Moore to dine out with us and see the show. The river was a raging, impassable torrent under a cloudless sky and a clear moon and the only thing to do was to cut our losses and go home to bread and cheese. But the night we were invited to dinner at Government House and it poured with rain all day was a different matter. I drove down at five o'clock to inspect the Sasaa and it was obviously impassable, certainly by car, perhaps even by truck. But a dinner invitation to Government House is by way of being a royal command; one cannot just not turn up. And we have no telephone, a fact which the denizens of Honiara can never quite grasp. So we decided to take the big truck, and mobilised a few labourers and houseboys to push us out of rivers if need be,

'In Journeyings Oft . . .'

bribing them with the price of seats at the cinema. We put on our best dining-out clothes, except for the shoes, waded out into the mud and cautiously climbed aboard. The escorting party, delighted at the prospect of an evening on the town for nothing, sang noisily all the way, jumping down at every river and wading through to test the depth and establish the best route. We arrived a little late, saying to each other, 'I bet we'll have the only *lorry* in Government House car park.' We were lucky to get as far as the car park, for the guard on the gate regarded our rowdy party with the deepest suspicion, thinking perhaps that the people's revolution had broken out, and would not at first admit us at all. Eventually, catching sight of Eric's dinner jacket, they acknowledged us as *bona fide* guests, but they insisted that our noisy crew should disembark and wait for us, on our return journey, outside the gate. We then slunk into the darkest corner we could find where we struggled furtively into our shoes and the remainder of our evening dress before emerging, immaculate, smiling and British, before the critical eye of the ADC in the well-lighted entrance hall.

By and large, however, one increasingly asks oneself, 'Is your journey really necessary?' and tends not to make it if it is not. Things rarely turn out as one had hoped, as on the Sunday when Eric was due to preach at a festival evensong at the cathedral and we planned to stay on in town and have a quiet hotel meal afterwards. But Honiara proved to be swarming with our students, who had gone in on the truck to the earlier feast and suffered multiple punctures, which left the truck hopelessly incapacitated until the garage opened on Monday morning. We never had our quiet hotel meal; indeed we never had a meal at all but spent the evening trying and failing to improvise transport for 'olgeta' and then finding somewhere for the stranded to sleep. This we regard as wholly typical of our transport arrangements and when we think of England now we contemplate possible suburban vicarages and say to each other with the deepest appreciation, 'And a corporation bus passes the front gate.'

XIII

HONIARA

What is so special about Honiara, that goal of all our journeys? It is the biggest town in the Solomon Islands (population in 1970, 11,200; the other two towns, Auki and Gizo on other islands having populations of about 1,500 each) and growing fast. It is strung out along six or seven miles of a coastal road and up on the ridges behind, for the hills come down quite rapidly at this point to the sea. To English ears this may not sound much more than an outsize village, but when you consider that 90 per cent of the Solomon Islands people live in rural areas in communities ranging from 20 to 200 people, Honiara really does represent the bright lights.

The centre of the town is Point Cruz, so named by the Spanish explorer Mendana who landed here briefly in 1568 and set up a cross, then sailed away; when he returned to the area thirty years later, he could not even find the island he had named Guadalcanal, which did not get back into world history until the Second World War when the Americans made a stand here and, after fierce and bloody fighting on sea and land, turned back the Japanese advance in the Pacific. The coast is still strewn with rusting heaps of metal which were once destroyers and landing craft. Wrecked aircraft are still proudly cherished in the coastal villages and when the Honiara town council digs beneath its road for drains or electric cables the workmen sometimes turn up the odd skeleton of an American or a Japanese soldier. No wonder 'the War' is the defining moment in history for the Solomons people and old war films still retain their popularity at the cinema.

Honiara

Honiara was founded on the airstrip and the few miles of road that the Americans installed and the Qonset huts they left behind them. To this day, several of the major stores are housed in these Qonset huts; so is the cinema and the Roman Catholic cathedral. We sometimes think, indeed, that the Qonset hut has exercised a permanent influence on the local architectural style, for when one of the prosperous Chinese traders of the town decided recently to pull down his barns and build greater, we were astonished to see rising from the ground a new store which was, in effect, yet another Qonset hut.

Other and pleasanter buildings have been put up. The new Government House is pleasing and so is the post office. The new community centre is quite an exciting building which puts me in mind of a tall ship. It is partly open to the sky and when a dance is held there some of the decorations are ready-made in the form of banana-trees. The museum has achieved a very attractive blend of traditional style with permanent materials and has a beautiful courtyard. At the time we arrived, the Anglican cathedral was still in its Qonset hut but this has been pulled down to make room for diocesan offices and other buildings while a most beautiful new cathedral has been put up a mile away, spacious, cool and open-sided. It is embellished with some remarkable local works of art including the inevitable shell decoration but also the only example I have ever seen anywhere in the world of what you might call Our Lady of the mini-skirt, a most lovely figure in wood which depicts Mary as a Melanesian schoolgirl, bareheaded and in a simple short frock. The other new Anglican church of All Saints in the central commercial district also has a simple beauty but it received from a distant island what I can only regard as an unfortunate, if loving, gift from an enthusiastic, and indeed expert, carver. More than life size, it purports to be an effigy of the late Bishop Alfred Hill, an Englishman who died in 1969. The figure is in ebony wood, lavishly decorated with shell-work, which would be tolerable perhaps in the trimmings

China Town, Honiara

Honiara

of the cope and mitre but when it comes to the finger nails and the teeth. . . . It was intended as a lectern, with the book-rest growing, as it were, out of the shoulders of the figure so that the reader was forced to lurk invisible behind the late bishop's mitred head uttering oracles like a priest with a bull-roarer at a heathen shrine. The whole thing proved too much for the gravity mainly of officiants at services and the good bishop was ultimately banished to the doorway where he stands – quite in the manner of the tutelary deities at the entrance of 'custom' houses – a rather sinister figure, especially at night when the false teeth grin out at the passer-by and the finger-nails take on the aspect of claws, gleaming in the casual illumination from nearby shops. It is all a million miles from the bishop as I remember him on the one occasion we met, a rather conventional person with a slightly plummy but very public-school voice, an ex-sea captain and very, very British.

The commercial buildings, with the exception of the two banks which have done their modest best, are not beautiful and most of them are hardly seemly for what must be regarded as a capital city. A good deal of the shopping area is 'China Town' which stretches along the Metaniko River at the point where it crosses the road and flows sluggishly into the sea. The Chinese stores are mostly unpretentious shacks in various makeshift materials, largely corrugated iron. They bear names such as 'Wong Pew, Yipyuk Store', and 'Ho Kee' (universally pronounced 'hockey', all, no doubt, barbarously anglicised as in the case of 'Sweeties', or even the renowned 'Joy Store'. The Joy family has greatly prospered as manufacturers of ships' biscuits and then bread, on the strength of which they eventually opened a very successful supermarket. This was in its early days when we arrived in 1969 and it was generally known as 'The Joy Biscuits' but not to us newcomers. Consequently we were somewhat startled when the Bishop's then secretary, a rather excitable young Englishman, telling us about a quarrel he had witnessed which came to blows, solemnly concluded, 'And he hit him in the Joy Biscuits.' The name has had an

Within a Chinese emporium

Honiara

anatomical reference in our household since then – not exactly a punch on the nose but a blow in the joy biscuits.

Within these Chinese emporia, there is a remarkable jumble of merchandise from ships' stores and fishing tackle to sewing cotton, tin baths, mattresses and enamelware and – if you know where to look and can succeed in communicating with the Chinese storekeeper or his womenfolk – things like sandalwood chests and ivory Mah Jong sets with instructions in Chinese. It all needs rather more time and energy than one ever has to spare and one is often puzzled to find necessities at the time one needs them. Many things come (and almost immediately go) with each arrival of the *Papuan Chief* from Australia and we have learnt to watch out for these brief bonanzas and make a special trip, rivers permitting, on what we hope will be the most favourable day after the ship has discharged her cargo. But all too often one will be told – especially if one is looking for something urgently required such as a spare part for a broken-down grass-cutter or a reel of sewing cotton or sometimes, dire catastrophe for Australians, a supply of bottled beer – 'It's on the wharf', where it often stays for weeks, if not months. No wonder material goods of all kinds are frequently referred to as 'cargo'. I even have a fleeting sympathy with some of the cargo cultists of New Guinea (happily we do not have them here) who expect God to supply them, on some day of eschatological bliss, with all the cargo they need from a heavenly ship. Indeed, on our first visit to Sydney, I looked eagerly up to see if a heavenful of cargo was, as is reported, situated immediately above that great city and half expected the skies to rain tinned meat during the apocalyptic thunderstorm which greeted our arrival.

But shopping in Honiara is improving all the time. In 1969, local residents would take one on a Saturday morning to a spot between the road and the sea where a few women sat under trees selling a few tomatoes. They have increased in number and the town council has built a market shed on the spot and it is now possible on most days of the week to buy local fruits

Married to Melanesia

and vegetables – bananas, pawpaws, limes, pineapples, tomatoes, shallots, aubergines, beans and green peppers – in Honiara market, though I am so well supplied at home by 'ravens' that I rarely need to do so. We are amused to notice that the market traders behave exactly like the 'ravens' (they are the same people of course), selling everything in ten cent – 'one shilling' – heaps or bundles; change is not given. I once went into the market with nothing smaller than a dollar note and nobody would change it; we think that nobody trusted himself (or herself) to count. The Solomon Islanders are far and away the most uncommercial people I have ever known; one feels that they venture into the modern world as sheep among wolves.

The market area has also a dairy with a 'mechanical cow' which dispenses more or less fresh milk (made up from powder by some process not domestically available), and sells ice cream. Next door is the fish shop, another new development, which sells local fish reasonably cheap. Most of it is bonito, which is brown and tough and tastes more like meat than like fish but is highly nutritious. The shop has lately branched out to include a fish-and-chips department, complete with salt and newspaper; and this is indeed a public benefaction in a town full of young men with jobs but still without brides (till they are sent over from their home islands) or proper cooking arrangements. An alternative to lunching at the hotel is now to buy fish and chips and consume them discreetly with the fingers in the botanical gardens, a delightful and usually deserted pleasance behind the prison, with a stream running through it – a place we would like to visit far oftener than we have time to, if only to satisfy our botanical curiosity by reading the labels on the trees.

Normally, however, on long shopping trips or still longer car-servicing trips, we lunch on the open terrace on the seaward side of the Mendana Hotel, on which one can sit undisturbed for a couple of hours: waiting for the town to rise from its siesta while looking across at Gela and thanking God one is not just about to cross the sea which is, at that hour, usually rising rather angrily, and watching any shipping and

Honiara

contemplating all around the tourists, mostly American, in their 'resort clothes'. We discovered the joys of the hotel in our Siota days when visits to Honiara were rather to be dreaded, what with the discomforts and uncertainties of the voyage and the certain discomforts of the town itself. Worst of these was the diocesan transit quarters (now somewhat reformed) where one could have a noisy room with two iron beds (bring your own sheets) and access to an inevitably grubby showerbath with cold water. There were also some alleged cooking facilities but we tended to eschew these when we found that if they worked at all they were as liable to electrocute the cook as to cook the food, and settled for eating at the hotel. The horrors of the transit house were aggravated by the fact that one had no transport, having arrived by ship, and it was up a steep and exceptionally rugged hill, calculated to make any physical trouble one had come over to get treated several times worse. On one occasion I came over alone and, for once, in good health and prepared to enjoy myself if possible as well as doing the necessary college and domestic business. I had just had an unexpected cheque from England and Eric has said, 'Treat yourself to a bit of comfort', so when the ship docked and some sort of diocesan transport met it I said – rather sheepishly, for I knew this was not pukkha missionary behaviour – 'Take me to the Mendana Hotel, please.' But oh the shame! The hotel was full up – any Honiara resident could have told me that it always is – and I had to appear as usual at our deplorable transit house begging for admission.

Meals, however, we always took at the hotel and I now regret that I never quite had the face to follow the example of Lily Best, the lady of the 'looless luggers'. She had been in the WREN and learnt to look after herself in trying circumstances, so, after inspecting the transit quarters, she took not only her meals but her baths at the hotel. 'Lovely hot water', she said to me, 'I *always* take my sponge bag and towel when I go to dinner there.' No one dared say Lily nay, I imagine, but the hotel *does* have its standards of propriety, especially in the

Married to Melanesia

evenings. For some years it displayed the enigmatic notice: 'Minimum dress requirements for gentlemen after 6 p.m.: long socks.' One was always tempted to incite some gentleman to try it out.

Night life, however, hardly exists in our capital city. We have an occasional evening meal out, usually lumbered with a two-ton truck in which we have driven students for eye-tests at the establishment of a remarkable Chinese optician who, being also a laundryman, dry-cleaner, barber and ladies' hairdresser, only puts his optician hat on after dark on Wednesday evenings. But these meals have to be taken soberly and early, as we discovered one night when we went to see a patient in the hospital, came away at half past eight and could find nowhere in Honiara at all where we could eat or drink.

There is also the Quonset hut cinema which we have been to perhaps five times in four years. Melanesian audiences, compared with African ones, are very quiet and well-behaved, so one can hear the dialogue – or at least one could if the sound apparatus worked properly. As it is, one can only make much sense of films which are mainly visual or those of which one knows the script pretty well, such as *The Taming of the Shrew*, and every time we go Eric vows that he will never again subject his eardrums to such maltreatment.

Our most frequent port of call in Honiara, when all is said, is the Central Hospital, still known to the people in wartime language as 'Number Nine'. Eric insists that the derivation of the name is the army code-number for the pill for constipation, one of the only two remedies that old soldiers believe are ever dispensed to them. He thinks it came in through vulgar Australian influence and says – though I have not noticed this myself, being a lady – that knowledgeable Melanesians grin when you use the term. Knowing that the hospital is American in origin, I have always disbelieved this story and during a recent personal residence in Number Nine have questioned the oldest inhabitant staff who assure me, without a flicker of the eye, that this was Number Nine Field Hospital during the

Honiara

fighting in the war and the various dressing stations in the area were numbered one, two, three, and so on. The American Field Hospital still forms the core of the buildings, though there have been various additions and patchings up and improvisations generally; there is never enough money to do what is really needed, that is to build a new hospital. It lies between the road and the sea on what is a pleasant bay except in cyclone weather. One of the 1972 cyclones did it considerable damage, washing away, among other things, the entire private ward. This was a row of small rooms jutting out towards the sea with a rather pleasant veranda at the end where the walking wounded could take the sea breezes.

The private ward is devoted to paying patients, a category which included by definition all the European population. European food is, indeed, provided in it as a matter of course and seems to be acceptable to all except the Chinese. I once shared a ward with a Chinese woman who had just given birth and I was amazed at the constant processions of family – husband, mother, mother-in-law, grandmother, sisters, cousins, aunts and small children who arrived at hourly intervals from half past six in the morning until half past ten at night bearing bowls of steaming food. She appeared to eat the lot and kept herself going during the night on packets of biscuits. When she rose from her bed and went out, she still had the figure of a little girl.

The old private ward had the advantage of adaptability. After the rebuilding, only two rooms were provided, one male and one female, with the limiting effect that there is only space for three men and three women to be sufficiently ill to be hospitalised in the private ward at any one time; one is encouraged to be, if possible, walking wounded and feels that being on the point of death or giving birth are the only reasonable excuses for occupying a bed. Europeans who have something major wrong with them but can travel are, on the whole, encouraged to 'go out' to Australia or New Zealand. In fact both Eric and I have had to 'go out' for surgery in the course

Married to Melanesia

of five antipodean years, though in my case I have twice been obliged to burden 'Number Nine' with my presence, in each case for several weeks, once with a slipped disc – long enough to get to know all its habits and its staff and to feel the oldest inhabitant. As hospitals go, it has been the pleasantest in my experience with a jolly, relaxed, rule-free attitude.

There are, of course, bigger public wards, male and female. a TB ward and a physiotherapy unit (of which I have also had personal experience) presided over by an American nun who collaborates with the only surgeon in the protectorate in a fantastic programme of rehabilitating polio victims. There were two major polio epidemics in the late forties and early fifties which left a trail of crippled people, now in their thirties and forties, who have been dragging themselves round their villages, often on their elbows, since childhood. Mr Cross, the surgeon, has become fascinated by this problem and the possibility of setting some of them on their feet, to the point of complicating his already over-burdened professional life by seeking them out and persuading them to undergo surgery. Sister Jane's physiotherapy unit is one of the happiest and most hopeful places in Honiara; one sees before one's eyes men and women who have had the necessary surgery struggling to their feet after twenty years and achieving even the modest freedom of crutches and calipers.

When we are not ill ourselves, we always have somebody to visit at the Central Hospital or, at the very least, somebody to bring to the outpatients' department or to see the only dentist in the country, so the truck – and our car – automatically turn their noses in the direction of Number Nine when they sight Honiara. Considering the general backwardness of the islands, I have always been struck by the confidence the people have in scientific medicine and the lengths they will go to in order to get people to the hospital. I find this a tribute to the real care and trouble that is taken by an overworked staff with inadequate equipment, always short of space and sometimes of drugs. They work very hard, dealing not only with the ills of the

Honiara

people of Honiara and Guadalcanal, but with a constant stream of emergencies, people brought in half dead, often after accidents, either by sea or, sometimes, by chartered light aircraft or helicopter. They are consistently cheerful, but always extended beyond the reasonable limits of their resources and always short of money.

There is only one surgeon, who actually flies around to the two other towns every month. If your surgical emergency occurs during his perfectly warrantable absence, it can be just too bad. It is also advisable to time one's misadventures to match the annual programme of visiting specialists who come up from Australia largely out of the goodness of their hearts, though their Government pays their expenses, as a form of aid to us citizens of a developing country. Gynaecological troubles, for instance, should occur in June or July, whereas eye troubles are best in April or May; if your cataract is not ripe for surgery in the right month, you will have to wait another year.

I had occasion one year to see for myself the major effort mounted for the visit of a team of eye specialists (Australian and Chinese) who came up from Melbourne and I marvelled that the hospital was able to do anything else that week. For some time before they arrived the population had been alerted on the radio to this opportunity and the nurses and medical assistants in the country districts were actively rounding up potential patients and arranging for their transport to Honiara. The morning I was in the queue myself, the whole hospital swarmed with people, many of them blind or half-blind, elderly, bemused by the big city, some unable to understand what was said to them – necessarily in pidgin, which old women in villages do not understand. Many were illiterate and this made the work of the local staff who were trying to do a preliminary screening eye test even more difficult. The old lady ahead of me could neither read nor speak pidgin. Another patient, a young man who spoke her language, jumped in to translate. The nursing sister was trying to use a test devised for the illiterate which involved moving geometric shapes on a

Married to Melanesia

set of cards, but this had to be explained in words and the translator had a very comprehensible urge to *show* the old lady what to do, thereby doing the test himself and throwing no light at all on the state of her vision.

Another patient was an old man in a wheelchair, clutching a stick and an unwieldy bag of personal belongings from which he refused to be separated. He was seen by the specialist and told to return the next day for surgery. I marvelled at the sheer patience and kindliness of the young (male) nursing trainee who was gentling him along, looking after his stick and his dirty old bundle, trying to find a place for him to sleep, talking to him cheerfully and he himself showing no sign of irritation under the extreme pressure of 'busy-ness', crowds of people, shortage of space and more than the usual degree of heat and humidity.

Ever since this occasion, I seem to have been coming across village acquaintances, such as Luke, wearing new glasses (identifiable by a small brand-label in the corner of one lens which nobody seems to bother to scratch off) and saying, 'Me see good now', sometimes adding, 'This fellow doctor emi cut eye belong me.' Very satisfied customers.

The hospital corridors are always full of child patients – there is no separate children's ward – wandering about, learning to walk again after orthopaedic surgery, liking to be talked to and addressing one as 'Sister'. Matron sometimes gives them balloons to play with and one sees them rushing madly about on their crutches and callipers, chasing each other and their lost balloons and one wonders what will happen to their plaster (known to them and their parents as 'concrete') if they fall, but the whole scene is immensely cheerful and friendly and somehow typical of life in the Solomon Islands where, after a year or two, one begins to feel that the whole place is a village and everybody knows everybody else and anybody's children are everybody's concern. Even in Honiara, which – to hear some Solomon Islanders talk – one might think was the ultimate in big city wickedness.

XIV

CHANGE

In my beginning is my end. Our arrival in the Solomon Islands was the culmination for us of a series of personal changes so violent and numerous as to be traumatic. Now, looking back over our five Melanesian years, what strikes me most is change again, change in ourselves and above all change in our work and our students, change in Solomon Islands society.

Standing back and looking at it, it is obvious enough that marriage in one's late forties is in itself enough to digest for two people who have already put in half a lifetime of energetic activity as independent and mobile single people. In our personal lives, I suppose, the biggest change has been that we finish our five island years convinced that we are married. Perhaps circumstances helped rather than hindered. I remember that we had one of our very infrequent rows – what over, I have no idea – when we were both near the end of our tether at Siota and I said, 'If it weren't for all this damned sea, I'd go back to my mother – if I had a mother', and was so struck by the absurdity of the whole Robinson Crusoe situation that I could not go on being angry.

I myself would probably have found it difficult in any circumstances to accept a new role in which I would be defined by most people as my husband's wife. It would, however, have come easier in a society less male-dominated than that of the Solomon Islands; also, if I had been able to exercise my own profession independently of my husband I think I should have felt less frustrated. Even now, fully accepted I believe as a teacher, I have my moments of resentment when I feel taken

Married to Melanesia

for granted as 'Mrs Warden' (which is what some of the students call me in charmingly Teutonic style), a mere woman, rather less than a professional and, of course, unpaid. From this point of view, I could hardly have made the transition from professional woman to wife more difficult for myself than by marrying a missionary whose own pay, by definition, bears no relation to his value or responsibility. (We have, indeed, never lived on it entirely, though we could have done so at a pinch.) There was never any question of my own professional work being paid for, a fact I knew quite well and accepted, as, indeed, we both accepted our general economic position quite happily in the context of working with and for a very poor people. What I had not realised was the difference an independent pay cheque makes to any worker's self-respect and there have been times when I have wondered whether anybody but myself cared about the quality of my work since it would make no economic difference to anybody whether I did it or not. I certainly never contemplated giving it up. It gave me a personal stake in the – very difficult – job we both felt we had undertaken and the work was, in any case, my own sort of thing.

Eric too must have had many personal adjustments to make to matrimony as well as to his role of theologian-cum-boy-scout; nobody can change his entire way of life at our age without something of a jolt. We have survived, however, and even enjoyed ourselves, if sometimes a little grimly, and we are clearly different people as a result of the experience from those who arrived in February 1969 on the temporary airstrip in Honiara.

There have been other changes in our attitudes and habits. I, at any rate, have sorted out a lot of essentials from inessentials. When I arrived at Siota I found it hard to believe that any serious education could be going on with such very poor equipment. We had, as it happened, stayed with a friend and former colleague of mine in the United States on our way here and been shown over the college in which he was teaching.

150

Change

We were very impressed with 'the plant' which was far superior to anything we had known in Africa or Fiji or even England. The contrast was extreme with the little huddle of frail leaf huts we found on the isolated sea coast of Gela. When we moved to Guadalcanal, things were at first even worse. There was a period when Eric and I were teaching in separate corners of our own still unfinished little house, within earshot of another class in the old, tumbledown chapel five yards away, and with the office filing cabinets and safe in our bedroom. Later, we got the villagers to run us up a set of leaf huts for tutorial rooms, where we assembled our small seminar groups and sat dispensing wisdom like so many Desert Fathers in the wilderness. I have taught in one of these huts holding an umbrella over my head to keep off a downpour and with the legs of my chair sinking into the wet earth floor. The huts were replaced, before they collapsed in a cyclone, by a permanent block of tutorial rooms; and indeed one of the more obvious changes at Kohimarama is that we now have a set of modest but adequate buildings. But I am bound to admit that real education has been going on all the time in surroundings which I regarded as impossible when I first arrived. We still have three leaf classrooms and the students are at this moment replacing an old, worn-out one with another like it. We are content with them; they are cooler than permanent buildings and we find them perfectly satisfactory for lectures, shabby as they look and dusty as they perpetually must be from the boring insects.

My attitude to the people, I also realise, has changed, both to our own students and to the people one casually meets. I had lived for fourteen years in West Africa and was used to turbulence; I suppose that is the fact. Melanesians struck me at first blush as dour and rather dull. They were, on the other hand, obviously much more virtuous as a people than the West Africans. In Accra, I twice had my handbag stolen from the seat beside me in my car by clever teamwork on the part of two young thieves, one of whom distracted my attention with conversation while the other made off with the bag; on one of

Married to Melanesia

these occasions I was actually robbed in a traffic jam and the (Ghanaian) driver of the car behind me saw the whole episode, jumped out of his car and gave chase, causing an even worse jam. In Honiara, I found, you could forget your purse in the car or leave it in a shop and nobody would touch it. All the same, I missed the excitement and the sharp-witted rogues, the repartee and the quick changes from anger to laughter. Especially, I missed those vast, laughing, quarrelling, economically powerful West African 'market mammies' and found the Melanesian women – little, quiet, ill-dressed and totally unflamboyant – a poor exchange. But I have learnt to appreciate and like the people we live among. I quickly realised that they were, though small, immensely tough and immensely hardworking. They are also honest, given neither to exaggeration nor flattery. I think, however, that their most admirable characteristic is an almost universal freedom from covetousness. This must be one of the few places in the world where tipping is not expected and I should be astonished to hear of a Melanesian involved in bribery and corruption, though not very surprised at public money disappearing through incompetence and – basically – lack of great interest in it. We always find that you can never be quite sure that anybody can count; I was recently told that some of the local languages count '1, 2, 3, 4, 5, a lot'. Another noticeable characteristic is the absence of much spirit of competition. People on the whole seem reluctant to stand out from the crowd or do better than their neighbours. This seems likely to create many problems in finding the necessary leadership for an independent country, but it is founded, I think, in a very healthy reluctance to disturb the comfortable values of an egalitarian society and one cannot help wishing the Melanesian people luck in resisting the emergence of an alienated proletariat.

When I think of our students, the change again is partly in my own attitude, but there certainly has been a very big change in them and this to us seems the most notable difference of all from 1969. All students everywhere in the world have to overcome a reluctance to think strenuously – don't we all? – but

Change

some are easier to stimulate than others. My West African pupils were always ready for a joke or an argument and I was deeply depressed when I arrived at Siota to find 'students' who seemed to regard seriousness and a sort of passive obedience as all that could reasonably be required of them. On the whole, they did not ask questions and if I tried asking questions of them there was an unspoken but implied response, 'You're the teacher, you ought to be telling us.' The level of verbal communication was, furthermore, so low that it was almost impossible to jolly things along with jokes. Both parties became equally frustrated and many were the long silences while I sat gazing out to sea, determined not to proceed until some sort of response was forthcoming.

All this has changed and for various reasons. An energetic staff of seven can obviously do more than one of two and by reducing the emphasis on lectures and increasing the requirement of individual reading and writing followed by discussion, the students have been forced to take more mental initiative and most of them have found that they liked it. We have never had a repetition of an incident George Connor described when a fairly recently ordained priest returned to Siota practically in tears, declaring that he would never be able to preach another sermon. When asked why not, he explained that the rats had eaten all his college lecture notes.

Our students have always taken responsibility for organising their gardening, pig-keeping, building, and so on themselves and it has always been well done. Then, after two years at Kohimarama, we had a curriculum conference with some outside help, in which we tried to get students and staff together to reshape the entire curriculum and make it a more meaningful preparation for the work our graduates would be doing in the real circumstances of their country. The changes actually made in the curriculum were, in fact, rather timid, but what did come out of the conference was a clear desire for student power, real power. This is perhaps the biggest change we have seen – and the most welcome. Eric used to describe the situation when we

Married to Melanesia

first arrived as 'Yes, Father, no, Father, three bags full, Father', and found it depressing as too submissive to be genuine. Now the place really is run by a monthly college meeting of the entire student body plus all the staff, any wives who care to come and, I have noticed with interest, occasionally our David. The president is a student 'moderator' elected for the whole year. An agenda is prepared in advance, consisting of anything anybody wishes to put on it. Anything can be said or asked; questions about money – how much have we? where does it come from? for what purposes? – are freely canvassed and people really do speak their minds either in English or in pidgin. It is in these meetings, more than in any of the classes or tutorials, that I have felt the spirit of life and independence that we have so much longed to see, and this is the biggest change of all in our time.

We meet in the library after supper on the first Friday of the month and the walls are plastered with what the students will insist on calling 'agendas' in the form of wall-posters. Some of them are very mysterious; but the meaning usually comes out in the course of discussion when one also senses certain 'hidden agendas' which can sometimes be coaxed to the surface. Eric gives a regular 'warden's report'; otherwise, most of the talking is done by the students. Food – as with students everywhere – makes a frequent appearance on the agenda and we have been interested to see a more discriminating attitude to eating gradually emerging. I always thought that the Melanesians were the first people I had ever met who were without a cuisine. Meals are taken at speed and with the utmost casualness; nobody seems to mind if a hot meal is eaten cold or lukewarm. The basic food is boiled kumara. (David, accustomed in my kitchen to frying, roasting, grilling, and so on, will enquire what is to be done with the potatoes and if I say 'Boil them', he replies, 'Just cook?', clearly indicating what 'cook' means to him.) The kumara will be eaten, hot or cold, often with tinned meat or fish mashed and warmed up in coconut milk, but not necessarily at a family or community meal. To the European eye,

Change

meals look like a perpetual and often peripatetic picnic. Fruit is eaten – but probably not in the course of a meal, more often while wandering about. Even at feasts the eating never goes on for more than ten minutes and I have witnessed a 'feast' (on the occasion of a land transfer) when nobody sat down to eat at all but the food was shared out among the various parties and carried off to their homes.

So the grumbles about food in the past always took the form of a complaint about the quantity of the rations or the quality of the rice or the inequitable distribution as between the families and the single men, never about the cooking. Lately, however, I have been delighted to hear suggestions and observations about the cooking itself. We employ a cook, who is virtually a not very bright labourer detailed for the job. College meetings are now saying, 'Can't we have a better cook?' or, 'Couldn't we send him on a course to learn something?' They are also saying things such as, 'Can we afford to buy some onions to make the food more interesting?' or, 'The bread baked on Friday is practically uneatable by Monday breakfast-time. Can we have ships' biscuits instead?' This may seem an immensely tedious way of discussing catering and budgeting, but it seems the Melanesian way; they do not really like leaving it to a committee. So we hammer out the facts and the numbers and multiply and divide our dollars and cents and finally decide, in the words which have become popular since the curriculum conference, to 'have a go'. This willingness to try new things out is another of the really big changes we have seen.

Items about food will be mixed up with more academic matters. The meeting will discuss whether Greek should be retained as an optional study in the college course. People will get up and say they cannot do it and hate trying. Others will say they like it. It will be pointed out that anybody going on to study for a theological degree will need it and in the end some decision will be reached. It will be a real decision and will be acted on.

The meeting will then pass on to a mysterious motion 'That

155

Married to Melanesia

we have no *lius* at Kohimarama' ('liu' is the local word for layabouts in Honiara – school-leavers who cannot find the jobs they want for the most part) and the staff will listen with interest, not knowing that we had any. The debate is highly allusive, held in very rapid pidgin, and seems to be generating a lot of heat. Furthermore, the Malaitamen are clearly on the opposite side from the Isabel men. Eventually it comes to light that a relation of somebody's wife has been seen hanging around the place, nothing has actually been stolen but a lot of the single men do not like the look of him; somebody wants to call the police, others want the warden to speak, others object to any action at all. The man whose wife is related to the alleged liu makes a speech so allusive as to be incomprehensible to me, but the people concerned understand it all right. Then the whole discussion fizzles out; we cannot be sure what has happened or will happen, but the matter has been resolved and the community is mysteriously satisfied. Which is more than it would be if the warden had been left to deal with the situation.

We then pass on to something that turns out to be sheer light relief: the condition of the college's fishing net. The net was bought (they are quite expensive) several months earlier after prolonged debate about the contribution it might make either to recreation or food supplies and Job was made fisher-king. Job is a third-year student, one of the older married men with several children and some years' experience as a catechist. He had polio in his youth and limps, but is nevertheless extremely agile and is, in fact, the college's best football coach and referee. His contributions to any debate are highly oratorical and accompanied with much gesticulation and on this occasion he seemed to be denouncing the community for neglect and maltreatment of the net. A hot argument developed in the course of which many technicalities were bandied about, Job emotionally asserting his ultimate authority over the net. Nets were part of his life, he had always had to do with nets, he knew exactly how to manage nets, his father and all his relations were expert with nets. In the course of the tirade, I under-

Change

stood him to say at one stage that he was born in a net. His point was felt to be made; everybody suddenly subsided and one sensed that the net would be properly looked after henceforward.

What to do with a year's church collections is the next 'agenda' and the surprising decision is to divide the money between a subscription to a local fund to provide the expenses (mainly warm clothes) of a party of Solomon Islands dancers going to the opening of the Sydney Opera House and a contribution to the British charity *Help the Aged* (for use in Britain) on the grounds that 'We are always getting money from overseas and we would like to send them something in return'.

Then a long discussion about the community store, its management, stocks, profits, and how to use them. It is decided to buy a cow for the Bishop Patteson Day feast, after much discussion about whether we can afford it and all the other things we need to spend the store profits on. A long argument follows about the best source of cows, and ultimately a cow committee of four, one from each year, is elected and charged with the duty of going and looking at cows, selecting one, getting it slaughtered and brought home on the right day. (The river will run blood when they take it there and cut it up and do it into parcels for the ovens.)

Somebody raises the question of bad debts at the store. Credit is not now allowed, but when we first arrived on Guadalcanal four years ago the first student storekeeper imprudently let some villagers run up small debts. Only one – a matter of some twenty-four dollars – is still outstanding and the debtor, Sepo, is, in his way, a local notable. Some angry speeches are made and a committee of three appointed to go and take him by the throat saying, 'Pay me that thou owest!' But, most interestingly, one of our most individual students, Ellison, a man who has had hardly any formal schooling but has spent years in the Melanesian Brotherhood becoming eventually Head Brother, and then coming on to us to study, gets up. He is the best pidgin speaker I know (he is so good that I

Married to Melanesia

often cannot follow him) and is always listened to with well-deserved respect. He reminds the meeting of the demands of Christian charity and he deprecates any aggressive attitude. He points out that we want to be on good terms with our neighbours. The meeting gradually cools and the bad-debt collectors are given new terms of reference (and in fact the outcome is a friendly meeting with the debtor and a promise that he will pay us out of his next sale of copra).

Many more items may follow. Should Sunday sermons be in English or pidgin? How can we get basketball rings and nets made? Shall we start an experimental fishpond? Is there any hope of getting more pocket money from the diocese? All is discussed in detail. There is some voting, but a consensus is preferred to a majority decision and generally one is reached. It all takes a great deal of time and taxes everybody's nervous energy. At the end of the meeting we usually vote a time extension for the generator to allow everybody to get to bed by electric light, but the warden and his wife normally need longer (and a stiff drink) to get over it, so we light an oil lamp and sit up for a while asking each other what was so-and-so's hidden agenda, or simply laughing over the idea of Job being born in a net or some such absurdity. And at the end we retire to bed far more satisfied with the state of the community – slightly turbulent, always wanting something different, but basically reasonable – than we ever felt in the old authoritarian days.

One hopes that the changes I have just been describing in our student body have some real link with the changes that are taking place in the Solomon Islands community. This is not a book about politics or economics and I have made no mention of the very rapid changes in government structures which have been happening during our five island years. I have said nothing about the modest advances in general education which are being made, nor about the recent very significant enquiry into the wishes of the people with regard to education; this has revealed clearly that the Solomon Islanders do not want – and

Change

know they do not want – simply to follow other people's patterns. The country is changing; that is clear. It is very small and geographically very unmanageable and one wonders how economically viable it is. But the people have a will of their own and, naïve and innocent as they often seem, they are nobody's fools when it comes to fundamental values.

All this is interesting and important and we talk about it constantly both with each other and with our colleagues and students, but I have not written a book about it or even a chapter; I would not altogether presume to do so. I confine myself to something far more subjective, one middle-aged Englishwoman's impressions of life on two South Sea island mission stations in the early 1970s.

Change being what it is, I fancy I may have written a period piece. We must be among the last specimens of our kind, for the colonial and missionary era is vanishing before our eyes. The Solomons have always struck me as the absolute far end, both in space and time, of the British Empire. British colonial government had its undoubted merits, but its time is past and if, in our small way, we have through our influence on the young, done anything to give it a friendly shove along and off the stage, we depart well content, grateful for the tolerance and friendship of many Solomon Islanders and wishing them good luck in the name of the Lord.